The Way
We Lived

The Way We Lived

California Indian Reminiscences, Stories and Songs

Edited with Commentary by

Malcolm Margolin

Heyday Books

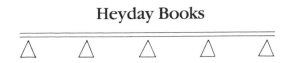

Published by Heyday Books
          Box 9145
          Berkeley, California 94709

ISBN: 0-930588-03-7 (hardcover)
ISBN: 0-930588-04-5 (paperback)
Library of Congress Catalog Card: 81-81383

Designed by Dennis Gallagher

Printed in the United States of America
10 9 8

Grateful acknowledgement is made to the following for permission to reprint
material copyrighted or controlled by them:

BEAR STATE BOOKS and FRANK F. LATTA for "I Am the Last" from *Handbook of Yokuts Indians* by Frank F. Latta. Copyright 1949 by Frank F. Latta; revised and enlarged edition copyright 1977 by Bear State Books.

WILLIAM BRIGHT for "Coyote's Journey" excerpted from *American Indian Cultural and Research Journal*, Vol 4, 1980.

CALIFORNIA HISTORICAL SOCIETY for "The Stone and Kelsey Massacre" by William Ralganal Benson, *California Historical Society Quarterly*, Vol 11, September 1932.

DUKE UNIVERSITY PRESS and WILLIAM J. WALLACE for "The Men I Knew" excerpted from "Personality Variation in a Primitive Society" by William Wallace in *Journal of Personality*, Vol 15 (4). Copyright 1947 by Duke University Press (Durham, N.C.).

MALKI MUSEUM PRESS and WENDY ROSE for "For the White Poets" from *Lost Copper* by Wendy Rose. Copyright 1980.

STEIN AND DAY for "A Man Without Family" from *Deep Valley* by B.W. and E.G. Aginsky. Copyright 1967 and 1971.

UNIVERSITY OF WASHINGTON PRESS for "A Great and Wise Shaman" and "I No Longer Believe" from *Primitive Pragmatists* by Verne Ray, Copyright 1963.

UNIVERSITY OF WISCONSIN PRESS and ELIZABETH COLSON for "My Grandfather" and "Crying" excerpted from *Autobiographies of Three Pomo Women* by Elizabeth Colson. Published by The Archaeological Research Facility, Department of Anthropology, University of California at Berkeley, 1974.

Y'BIRD for "I Remember" by Edward Montez and "long ago brown bears" by William Oandasan from *Calafia: The California Poetry* edited by Ishmael Reed. Copyright 1979.

Acknowledgements

I am, as always, immeasurably grateful to the partnership of Rina
Margolin whose ideas and standards suffuse the book.

Special debts of gratitude are also owed to: Amy Godine who collected
much of the material; Francine Hartman for help in the final stages of
editing and production; Donna Dumont for research and for contributing
many valuable ideas; Paul Velde for courageous and badly needed
editorial criticism; Christina Kessler for advice on both the writing and
the selection of photographs; Joan Feldman and David Sheidlower for
help in production and design; Vera Mae Frederickson who provided
guidance from the very beginning; and Jose Hatier for many hours of
conversation that broadened my understanding of Native American
thought.

I am also truly grateful to Larry Di Stasi, Rob Hurwitt, Bruce Kaiper,
Rebecca Kurland, Frank Lobo, and Randy Millikan for their critical
readings of the manuscript at various of its stages; and to Linda Tontini
and Celia Ramsay for their help in the latter stages of production.

Deepest thanks to Dennis Gallagher (book designer) for his kindly
cooperation, and to Georgianna Greenwood for the calligraphy on the
map.

I am further thankful to Dave Chamberlin of the Indian Action Library
in Eureka; the staff of the Bancroft Library in Berkeley; Frank Norick and
Gene Prince at the Lowie Museum of Anthropology; Peter Palmquist and
Erich Schimps of Humboldt State College; Mrs. Thomas of the National
Anthropological Archives at the Smithsonian Institution; and Elitha Rea
of the California State Museum Photographic Archives in Sacramento, all
of whom provided assistance in procuring the photographs. I'm especially
grateful to Gene Prince for guiding me through the Lowie Museum collection and for his extraordinary care in printing the photographs I
needed.

The hospitality of Christopher Weills, Sara Satterlee, and "Elizabeth"
shows on every page.

My heartfelt thanks to Robin Freeman and Berkeley Creators Associ-
ation; and to Red McClintock for his valuable advice.

Finally, the deeper I have gotten into California Indian studies, the
greater my debt has been to the University of California Press. Since the

turn of the century, the U.C. Press has been publishing primary source material, ethnographies, archaeological reports, and linguistic material in a number of different series. Without their long-term commitment to the field, the material available for an anthology such as this would have been meager indeed, and our understanding of the California Indian world would have been sadly impoverished.

Table of Contents

The Way
We Lived

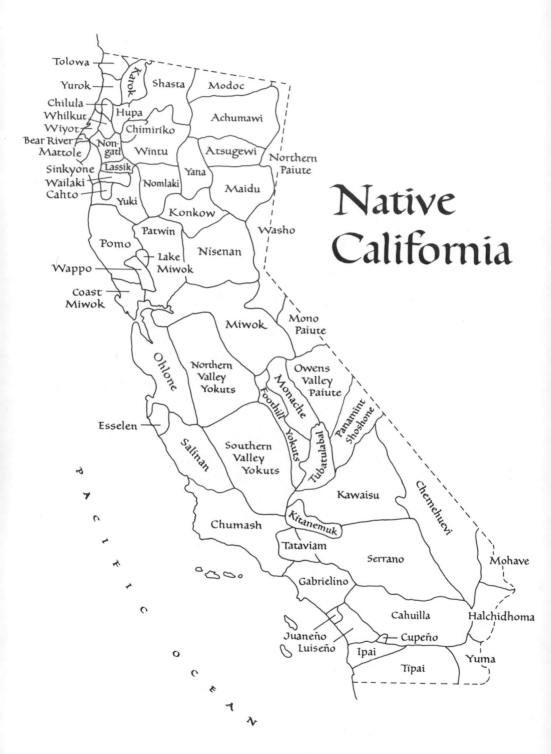

Tolowa
Yurok
Karok
Shasta
Modoc
Chilula
Whilkut
Hupa
Wiyot
Chimiriko
Achumawi
Bear River
Mattole
Non-gatl
Wintu
Atsugewi
Northern
Paiute
Sinkyone
Wailaki
Cahto
Lassik
Yana
Yuki
Nomlaki
Maidu
Konkow
Patwin
Pomo
Lake
Miwok
Nisenan
Washo
Wappo
Coast
Miwok
Mono
Paiute
Ohlone
Miwok
Northern
Valley
Yokuts
Owens
Valley
Paiute
Monache
Esselen
Foothill
Yokuts
Panamint
Shoshone
Salinan
Southern
Valley
Yokuts
Tubatulabal
Kawaisu
Chemehuevi
Chumash
Kitanemuk
Tataviam
Serrano
Mohave
Gabrielino
Cahuilla
Halchidhoma
Juaneño
Luiseño
Cupeño
Ipai
Yuma
Tipai

PACIFIC OCEAN

Native
California

Introduction

The following collection of reminiscences, stories, and songs reflects the diversity of the people who once lived in California—a diversity so enormous that it can scarcely be imagined today. Picture a typical spring afternoon in California two hundred years ago. On the prairies of the northeastern part of the state a man, hiding behind a clump of sagebrush, waves a scrap of deerskin in the air, trying to rouse the curiosity of a herd of grazing antelope and draw them within range of his bow and arrow. Along the Klamath River a boy crawls through the circular doorway of a large plank house and walks downstream to watch his father and uncles fish for salmon beneath the redwoods. In the Central Valley a group of women, strings of wildflowers in their hair, wade out into the deep sea of rippling grass to gather roots. As they push forward herds of elk scatter before them. In San Francisco Bay two men paddle a rush boat through the quiet channels of a saltwater marsh. East of the Sierra, families—eager for change and weighed down with burden baskets—leave their winter homes in the desert and trek through pine forests toward thawing mountain lakes and the promise of good fishing. At the edge of the Mohave Desert men and women plant corn, bean, and pumpkin seeds in the warm, fertile mud of the Colorado River.

Waves of people began migrating into California more than ten thousand years ago—bands of bold explorers perhaps, or maybe they were desperate and frightened refugees who had been ousted from homelands elsewhere. They came into California from many places and over the course of many thousands of years. One group spoke a language of the Algonkin family of eastern North America. Another group spoke an Athapascan language related to languages of Canada. There were speakers of the Uto-Aztecan or Shoshonean language family of the Southwest; speakers of the Hokan-Souian language family of the Great Plains; speakers of Penutian, whose linguistic relatives may have included the Tsimshian of British Columbia and perhaps the Mayans of the Yucatan; and at least one band of Yukian speakers whose language can be linked to no other surviving language in the world.

3

As group after group migrated into California, they gradually dispersed along the ocean beaches, settled into secluded mountain valleys, moved out into the open desert, and established villages in the oak savannahs of the Sierra Foothills. They built wooden houses in the redwood and pine forests, underground earthen houses in the grasslands of the Central Valley, rush and willow houses along the fringes of marshlands. Centuries, sometimes thousands of years passed, and people of the same language family lost contact with each other. Some became almost totally isolated within their narrow valleys, some merged with neighboring groups of different linguistic stock. As a result, when white explorers first set foot in California, they found over 120 languages being spoken, seventy percent of them as mutually unintelligible as English and Chinese. Stephen Powers, a nineteenth century ethnologist, complained of traveling for "months in regions where a new language has to be looked to every ten miles sometimes."

The great variety of languages was matched by a great variety of customs, technologies, beliefs, and physical characteristics. The Yuman people of southernmost California and the Modoc of the northern border were among the most warlike people in North America, while residents of the central part of the state were among the most peaceful. The Mohave who lived along the Colorado River were the tallest of all Native Americans, the Yuki of Mendocino County the shortest. Dances, religious practices, foods eaten and shunned—indeed, almost every aspect of culture varied widely throughout the state.

As one example of California's extraordinary diversity, consider the matter of boats. The Yurok at the mouth of the Klamath River made dugout canoes out of redwood logs—crafts of "wonderful symmetry and elegance," according to an early visitor, "the sides as smooth as if they had been sandpapered." These Yurok boats were blunt and sturdy, made to withstand the battering of ocean waves and the scraping of river bottoms. The Modoc, by comparison, made extremely delicate dugouts hollowed out to an amazingly thin shell—boats well suited to the calm waters of Tule and Lower Klamath Lakes.

The Chumash of the Santa Barbara Channel had a totally different concept of boatbuilding. They fashioned boats, sometimes over thirty feet long, out of thin planks. Lacking nails they drilled holes in the planks and sewed them together with thongs of deer sinew. Then they caulked the seams with asphaltum, painted the sides red with hematite, and decorated the bows with white sea shells. These were ocean-going vessels in which the maritime Chumash voyaged to the Channel Islands, Santa

Catalina, and even to remote San Nicolas Island sixty-five miles from shore.

The Choinimni, a Yokuts group of the San Joaquin Valley, bound tule (bulrush) together with willow withes to make barges fifty feet long. They outfitted these immense barges with bedding, baskets of acorns and dried meat, even clay-lined fireplaces. Firewood was taken aboard, and one or more families embarked onto the sloughs, waterways, and lakes of the Central Valley, for a combined fishing expedition and vacation that often lasted weeks.

Even this does not come close to exhausting the types of boats used in California. Dugouts were made in a variety of designs out of locally available wood: redwood, fir, cottonwood, juniper, and pine. Tule craft ranged from tiny floating platforms from which Tubatulabal fishermen hurled harpoons to thirty-foot boats that once plied Clear Lake carrying several persons or over a ton of freight. Some groups lashed logs together to make rafts. Others used large baskets or even clay pots—towed by strong swimmers—to ferry children and goods across a river.

The variety of watercrafts in California suggests the remarkable variety of people and culture. The people we call "Native Californians" actually belonged to over five hundred independent tribal groups. Such diversity boggles the modern mind, overtaxing our systems of categorization and nomenclature. Consequently we moderns have tended toward generalization. We refer, for example, to the "Pomo" as if there had once been a Pomo tribe or a Pomo culture. Before the coming of whites, however, the Pomo were several dozen independent tribal groups—small nations, as it were—each with its own territory and chief. Pomo groups who lived in the interior valleys differed widely in customs, beliefs, and languages from those who lived along the coast. The major justification for grouping such diverse people under a single name is that the languages they spoke— seven different, mutually incomprehensible languages—are linguistically related and of common origin.

Pomo, in short—like Miwok, Maidu, Yokuts, etc.—is largely a concept of our own invention. Nevertheless for over a hundred years stories and songs, accounts of daily life, baskets and other artifacts have been collected from people described simply as "Pomo." Also, as generations have passed, the unique identities, characteristics, territories, and sometimes even the names of the many independent tribal groups have become obscured. Thus this book has no choice but to follow the conventional nomenclature and refer to people as Pomo, Maidu, or Miwok, however misleading. In fact this book does something much worse. In the following pages mention is often made of "Native Californians," "California Indians," or of a "California" way of thinking or acting. California, of course, is our own way of defining the world; the area it describes holds together as a unit only in the modern mind. In terms of native culture, "California" is utterly meaningless. So be forewarned. References to California, even more than references to Pomo, are concessions to modern perspective and definition, rather than adequate descriptions of the incalculable human richness and multiformity that existed here two hundred years ago.

California is thought to have had the densest pre-Columbian population anywhere north of Mexico. In 1769, when the first Spanish colonists arrived, an estimated 310,000 native people were living within the borders of the present state. Then came the missions and the *ranchos*; the goldminers, loggers, and farmers; the silting of streams, clearing of forests, draining of marshes, fencing of grasslands, and elimination of game; the diseases, the hatred, and the violence; the unspeakable tragedy. By the beginning of the twentieth century fewer than 20,000 native people were left in the state.

After 1900 California's Indian population began to increase, but many of the survivors were children of mixed marriages and broken traditions. Those who spoke native languages and who remembered and valued native culture continued to decline. The twentieth century saw a steady, inexorable shrinking of witness to the old ways of life. Anthropologists and other scholars scurried among the survivors, trying to salvage what they could from those who still remembered. Carobeth Laird, wife of the linguist-anthropologist John P. Harrington, described the mood: "The vessel of the old culture had broken, and its precious contents were spilling out and evaporating before our very eyes. Harrington, like a man dying of thirst, lapped at every random trickle."

Harrington was not alone. Although it is dreadful how much has been lost—whole tribal groups have disappeared with scarcely a word recorded—it is nevertheless astounding how many Native Californian songs, stories, speeches, and reminiscences have been preserved: literally thousands of dictaphone cylinders, disks, records, and tapes; folders, boxes, and filing cabinets filled with field notes; and thousands upon thousands of pages of material published as monographs, books, or in scholarly journals.

It has been several years since I took my first plunge into this vast sea of linguistic and ethnographic material. I originally had, if I remember correctly, a rather lofty ambition. I planned a comprehensive survey of Native California literature—one which would be, if not complete, at least representative. As time went on the impossibility of the task gradually dawned on me. Not only was I overwhelmed by the mass and variety of material available, but much of that material was in itself simply bewildering.

How could I deal, for example, with the large number of "autobiographies" which gave no details about birth, marriage, or occupation, but instead consisted of meticulous recountings of dreams and contacts with the spirit world? Such autobiographies made perfect sense in a cultural context. Native Californians traditionally lived in small tribal groups in which the external details of each person's life were intimately known. It would never occur to a woman, for instance, to talk about how she made baskets, how she ground acorns, or who her children were, for such things were known by everyone. To mention them would have been too obvious—like mentioning the fact that she had two legs and a nose. The subject of autobiographies is what other people do not know—in this case the world of one's dreams and the nature of one's spirit-world contacts, which for most Californians was the most important and most individual aspect of their lives. Yet while I recognized that such dream and spirit autobiographies were typical and thoroughly indicative of the native thought process, I found the bulk of them so foreign to the modern experience as to be inaccessible to all but the most dedicated student. Thus in preparing this collection I tended to pass over most of such material in favor of those autobiographies that were less typical but were structured more in line with our own conventions.

Similarly many Indian stories and myths seem rambling and plotless by modern standards. Originally there was no real need for plot. After all, the entire audience—except for the very young children—had heard each story and myth many times. Since everyone knew the plot, the storyteller was free to concentrate instead on voice, cadence, and performance. Especially performance! Imagine, for example, a rainy winter night. People have crowded into the assembly house or large dwelling. A fire is lit—it crackles and smokes from the moisture in the wood—and the storyteller launches forth, voice rising and falling; now talking, now singing; adopting the tone of one character, then another; shouting, whispering, grunting, wheedling, laughing—and all in a language molded to the story by centuries of previous performances; all in an energized setting in which family and friends are crowded together.

Anthropologists, linguists, and folkloricists have painstakingly recorded and transcribed many stories. Yet when such stories are stripped of the richness of human voice and the presence of living audience, cut off from cultural knowledge and tradition, translated into a distant language and set into type, they are often so diminished that many of them seem formless, empty, and incomprehensible to us.

Songs in particular suffer in translation. The tune, the rhythm, the nonsense syllables, the very life is often pressed out of a song as it passes into written English. How can one even begin to translate a Maidu shaman's recital, described by a listener as a "tangle of breathing and blowing sounds, bilabial trilling, nonsense syllables, and esoteric utterances?" How can one capture songs in Lower Lake Pomo, a language full of hissing sounds and sharp clicks such as one finds in certain African languages? Indeed, how can one convey any song except to sing it? Once again a huge body of very typical material had to be passed over in my final selection.

Thus my plan to present a comprehensive, or at least representative survey of Native Californian literature quickly ran into trouble. In fact as time went on I strayed further and further from the goal, so that the reminiscences and stories, songs and speeches that follow—while thoroughly authentic and (as nearly as possible) true to tone—are basically a personal selection. Here, then, is what seemed to jump out of the mass of collected material, suddenly illuminating some aspect of native life, or presenting me with something that I found beautiful, tragic, terribly interesting, or simply funny. Here are the selections that transported me, for a few minutes at least, into another world—that made me feel what it must have been like to have been a shaman dancing for power, a young boy awaiting initiation, an old man gazing at a pine tree he could no longer climb, a young girl hearing for the first time the mourning cries of her mother, a member of an audience listening to Coyote tales in an atmosphere of shared laughter. Here are the selections that have filled me with wonderment and have given me a deeper understanding not only of Native Californians, but of all humanity.

I: Growing Up

Lively, lively, we are lots of people.

Maidu song

The Cradle*

A Native Californian child was born into a tightly-woven family, into a small tribal group, into a people whose lives were influenced by traditions many hundreds of years old. The men hunted the way their fathers, grandfathers, and great-grandfathers had hunted—indeed, they hunted in the very same meadows and woodlands, and the deer they stalked were the direct descendants of the very deer their forefathers had stalked. The women gathered basketry roots from the same sedge beds and in the same ways their mothers, grandmothers, and great-grandmothers had done before them. It was an ancient, intimately-known world into which an infant was born. A child in its lifetime would never be expected to improve or alter things—change was feared—but rather to fit in with the old ways, to adapt to its customs. This was a world in which innovation and independence were discouraged, and in which the prime virtues were obedience, moderation, and restraint.

Soon after a baby was born, it was swaddled tightly into a basketry cradle. There were practical reasons for restraining a child: California had grizzly bears, rattlesnakes, scorpions, poisonous plants, rushing water, and numerous other dangers. Also, a swaddled baby seldom cried or fussed. Yet surely those early months packed into a basketry cradle must have greatly influenced personality. The severe restriction of movement curbed independence and a sense of experimentation. A child *watched* the world rather than acted upon it. Perhaps in the process the child developed an attitude of acceptance toward the world—an attitude that throughout a person's life would be amplified by other cultural experiences, until in the end *acceptance of the world* would become the very center of a complex system of belief and value.

T hey have an extra basket for a child when it is born; an aunt might have given an old one, or a grandmother might have made one especially. They roll the inside bark of red or white willow (rich people use maple bark) into soft balls that they

---

*Tribal designations appear at the end of each selection. For information about sources and narrators, see notes beginning on page 201.

use as diapers. Layers of it are put in the baby's basket, and the baby is laid on it. The diaper material is changed; it might be washed once or twice but, if possible, clean material is used. They are always very particular to keep these things nice and clean. When the baby is first put into the basket, they have a peculiarly shaped rock as a pillow for the head. They keep it there for about a week and then take it away. The baby stays in the basket until he is old enough to crawl, and sometimes he crawls with the basket still on.   NOMLAKI

The rock pillow helped flatten the back of the baby's head, for in much of California a flattened head was considered a mark of beauty. Thus a child was from its first moments literally molded by cultural values. Indeed, the image of the baby crawling turtle-like with its cradle on its back describes not only the circumstances of California Indians, but the fate of all humanity. We may have been born free, but by the time we are ready to crawl we already bear the weight of our culture upon our backs— a culture which is at once our burden and our refuge.

My Grandfather

As a child grew older family members—often aunts, uncles, or grand-parents—undertook its education. The child received practical instructions in a variety of skills, as well as repeated lectures on being virtuous. On a deeper level the child absorbed (without quite realizing it) attitudes, manners, and values from the people around it. There was a right and wrong way of doing everything—of singing, of talking, of eating.

A Pomo woman, speaking broken English, gives an affectionate remembrance of her grandfather, a man who did things in the old manner—fastidiously and correctly.

Grandfathers don't teach much. Only "Don't run around with another man or married man. Be good to people. Be kind to people. Don't run around in the night time." That's what my grandfather said to me. Not to go to different houses; not to visit people. That's what my grandfather said, my mother's father. They don't teach much. But they tell you lots of stories, lots of old kinds of stories. How things happen, and how a person do long time ago. Sing some kind of song.

He was a great hunter, that old fellow. One time I saw him, he made traps for birds—all kinds of birds, for larks and quails and cottontails. He used to make old time traps. He used to put lots of them out in the evening. He used to have baskets and used to fill them up with the game: rabbits, cottontails, birds. He used to have all of them in the basket [traps], and next morning early he would go out to get them. And when he bring them home in the morning, he used to build a fire, and he take all the feathers off. He cleaned all the birds, and he cooked it. He was the only one got to cook it. None of us helped with that. And when we ate the bird, we never bite it or break the bone. We just pull the meat off with the fingernails. It would have made him have bad luck if we bite it and break the bones. That's the way we did things. He used to cook it on the coals. He had acorn mush and acorn bread too. Tastes good with acorn mush—cold acorn mush cooked last night and left to set overnight....

My grandfather said he put the deer head on [as a disguise] when he want to go out hunting. He used to go out among the deer. The deer wanted to smell his behind. He always just turn around and sit down. It used to make me laugh when he tell that story.

POMO

Learning to Hunt

Tipai and *Ipai*, words meaning "person" in the two major dialects of the Diegueño language, have come to denote the people who once occupied the desert area of extreme southern California and the northern portions of Baja California. Far from being a "tribe," the Tipai-Ipai consisted of thirty independent, semi-nomadic clans. Some clans were traditional allies, others were enemies. Each clan generally wintered in its own sheltered valley and as spring unfolded it followed the ripening plants higher and higher into the mountains, migrating back to the valley floors each fall.

Carelessness toward the animal world was severely disapproved of everywhere in California, especially among the Tipai-Ipai. Big game was relatively scarce in their arid environment, and a boy underwent a long and detailed training as a hunter. If he displayed proficiency and luck at hunting rodents, lizards, and other small game he would be taught to hunt rabbits. If successful at that he might eventually be trained to stalk deer and perhaps even mountain sheep. The hunting of big game animals fell under the close supervision of the clan's huntmaster, and was invested with considerable ritual and honor.

When I was a boy I always hunted with my father's younger brother. I remember when he first took me hunting. I had a small bow and arrows, little better than toys. My uncle told me to poke into a pack rat's nest with a long stick. I asked him instead to let me shoot when the rat sat outside, but he said, "No, you can't wound him." I insisted and shot, but the arrow failed to penetrate for lack of power. I cried and shuffled my feet in chagrin. My uncle told me that it was no use for me to try, anyway, because he would not let me eat it. "If you eat the rat, or anything you kill, you will have worms in your stomach." Up to the time I married I never ate what I killed. Others can eat the game, but a boy cannot eat his kill until he is adult. One who refrains is always lucky. When I was a grown boy, whenever I went to hunt, I killed several rabbits almost immediately.   TIPAI

From his first fumbling efforts as a child to the time he became an accomplished hunter, the Tipai youth was guided closely by tradition. For him—as for all California Indians—hunting was in no way a direct, primal confrontation between hunter and quarry. Rather the hunter throughout his life moved in a world complexly defined by ritual and custom.

The unmarried Tipai hunter was warned against eating the game he killed lest he get worms and bring bad luck upon himself. But the taboo had broad and important social consequences as well. It meant that as the youth grew in skillfulness he would not become independent; instead he would continue to provide food for his family, while his own meat would be supplied by his father, uncles, and older brothers. In this way family ties were maintained and even strengthened during adolescence. Even after marriage, when the hunter was free to eat what he had killed, he would continue to share his game with family, repaying those who had fed him during his apprenticeship and providing meat for younger brothers and nephews who were themselves just learning to hunt.

When a man was in his prime he probably gave more than he received, but when he reached old age, unable to get about easily, his membership in the clan would provide him with the fruits of a nephew's or grandson's first hunting. It was membership in clan and family—rather than individual skills—that provided one with identity and security.

A Man Without Family

Before the coming of whites the Sonoma and Mendocino County area held a diversity of people, among them the Pomo. Arts were highly developed, and indeed Pomo basketmakers have been considered among the most accomplished and sophisticated visual artists the world has ever seen. Ceremonial life, too, was immeasurably rich: secret societies, initiation rites, cult performances, shamans, festivals, and elaborate dances were a major part of life, suffusing everyday affairs with a strong sense of the sacred. The complexities of Pomo social, religious, and artistic life are fascinating. But underlying the complexities and elaborations was the institution of family, the solid foundation upon which Pomo life rested.

What is man? A man is nothing. Without family he is of less importance than that bug crossing the trail, of less importance than spit or dung. At least *they* can be used to help poison a man.

A man must be with his family to amount to anything with us. If he had nobody else to help him, the first trouble he got into he would be killed by his enemies because there would be no relatives to help him fight the poison of the other group. No woman would marry him because her family would not let her marry a man with no family. He would be poorer than a newborn child; he would be poorer than a worm, and the family would not consider him worth anything. He would not bring renown or glory with him. He would not bring support of other relatives either. The family is important. If a man has a large family and a profession and upbringing by a family that is known to produce good children, then he is somebody, and every family is willing to have him marry a woman of

15

their group. It is the family that is important....

The family was everything, and no man ever forgot that. Each person was nothing; but as a group, joined by blood, the individual knew that he would get the support of all his relatives if anything happened. He also knew that if he was a bad person the head man of his family would pay another tribe to kill him so that there would be no trouble afterward and so that he would not get the family into trouble all of the time. That is why we were good people. POMO

So deep did the sense of family go that the Pomo, in common with other Native Californians, tended not to view the individual as a complete, self-sufficient entity. *Family* was seen as the basic unit of humanity, individuals as mere components. A person isolated from family was grotesque, frightening, pitiful, and ultimately unable to survive—like a finger severed from a hand. Individuals were incomplete, transitory beings; only family persisted, only family had meaning and authority, only family could bestow complete personhood.

Puberty Dance Song

For girls, childhood ended with the first menstruation. In these tightly-knit family and tribal groups, the event was hardly a secret, but rather an occasion for public acknowledgement and elaborate ritual. Throughout most of California the girl's family—and in some cases the entire tribal group—might hold a coming-of-age feast and, in many places, a dance.

Thou art a girl no more,
Thou art a girl no more;
The chief, the chief,
The chief, the chief,
   Honors thee
In the dance, in the dance,
In the long and double line
Of the dance,
   Dance, dance,
   Dance, dance.   WINTU

Rolling Head

Throughout California menstruation was regarded as an important event. A menstruating woman was generally seen as unclean, defiled, even injured. At the same time menstruation gave her extraordinary magical powers, able to inflict illness or bad luck upon her enemies. Rituals were needed to restore the woman's "health" lest she come to harm and to neutralize her power lest she inadvertently bring harm to others.

Thus during menstruation a Wintu woman had to undergo a variety of restrictions: she lived alone for several days in a separate dwelling; abstained from meat, fish, and salt; refrained from sexual activity; and ate from special baskets and utensils. The first menstruation—the onset of puberty—demanded even more severe restrictions. For a full month the pubescent girl lived alone in a brush shelter several yards from the family dwelling. She struggled to remain awake for the first five days to prevent dangerous dreams. She ate nothing but acorn soup; she could not comb her hair or even touch her own body. She had to keep out of sight, and whenever she left the shelter to relieve herself she covered her head with a basket or deerskin lest a glimpse of her face bring bad luck to others.

The fears and rituals that surrounded menstruation—common everywhere in California—seem puzzling to us. We view menstruation as a relatively minor and decidedly personal occurrence. But in a society in which everyone was organically connected nothing was *personal*. The perceived dangers of menstruation affected not only the "moon-sick" woman, but other people to whom she was linked. A husband, for example, would not go hunting during his wife's menstrual period because her condition would affect his prowess and luck: after all, they were of the same family and thus connected as a unit. And a woman who was careless about her menstrual obligations, especially at puberty, would bring ruin not only upon herself, but upon her entire family—one of the underlying themes of the following Wintu "horror" story.

L ong ago people came into being and lived at a village; it was filled with people. People lived both on the flat on the west side of the river, and on the flat on the east side of the river too. There was a chief at the head of the people who had two daughters. The younger one reached puberty, but she did not tell her mother. However, her parents knew it. So they were to call a puberty dance, and they met and discussed it. In the evening the father spoke. "Early in the morning go strip bark for a maple bark apron," he said. "But don't take the girl who has reached puberty with you. Go secretly," he said.

The rest of the women got up early in the morning. They all went secretly, quite a little way north they went, and even some went north uphill and crossed the ridge to the north. Then later she woke up, the one who had reached puberty. And she went, though she was forbidden to go she went, going behind the others. She kept going until she reached them. Some were stripping bark and others already had much. She went right up to them and cut off maple bark.

All at once, she stuck her little finger with a splinter. It bled. Her older sister came up to her and wiped it with dead leaves. Then they said, "When will it leave off? The blood cannot stop flowing." And the rest of them all left, they knew already and were afraid so they left. She and her older sister were left behind alone. Some who had already gone reached the house and told the father. "She got stuck with a splinter while stripping bark," they said. And the old man said, "She does not listen to me."

She who had reached puberty, who was downhill to the north, now sucked blood and spat it out. Then more blood came and though she sucked the blood she could not stop its flow. Meanwhile the sun began to set. Until early evening she sucked, she kept on sucking, not being able to help herself. Then she got tired, not being able to stop it in any way. Suddenly she happened to swallow blood and smelled the fat. It tasted sweet. So now she ate her little finger, she ate it, and then ate her whole hand. Then she ate both her hands, devoured them. Then she ate her leg, ate both her legs. Then she ate up her whole body. Then her head alone was left and rolled about. She went rolling over the ground, her sister still beside her.

The old man in the house said, "From the north she'll come, she who went to strip maple bark. Put on your clothes, people. Get your weapons. We people are gone." And the people dressed themselves and got their weapons. And from the north they saw her come, she came rolling toward the house. She arrived in the early evening and lay there. After she had stayed there a while,

18

she bounced up to the west across the river to the flat on the west, where she threw the people into her mouth. She did not linger, she turned the village upside down as she devoured them all. Then she fell to the east across the river and lay there, and the next morning she threw those of the east flat into her mouth, ate them, devoured them all. Only her eldest sister she left for a while. And she went about the world, and when she saw people she threw them into her mouth and ate them. Each evening she came home, each morning she went about the world looking for people. Always she went searching.

One day she climbed up to the northern edge of the sky and looked all over the world, but she saw no one. So in the evening she came home, and the next morning she got up and threw her elder sister into her mouth. Then she came on her way, until she reached the edge of a big creek. She did not know how to cross. And from the other side she called. A man was sitting there. He threw a bridge over from the other side. She was crossing, and when she had gone halfway he jerked it, and it went down at Talat. And she fell into the river, and as she fell into the water a riffle pike jumped and swallowed her. And it is finished. That is all.   WINTU

Sand Painting Sermon

The Luiseño were a number of tribal-groups who lived in Southern California. Their villages—each with thatched conical dwelling houses, shade houses, a semi-subterranean sweat-house, and a fenced ceremonial enclosure (*wamkis*)—dotted the land from Mount Palomar to the coast. The Luiseño spoke a Shoshonean language, itself one of the Uto-Aztecan languages that flourished throughout the American Southwest, and indeed Luiseño culture (as well as Southern California culture in general) bears certain similarities to the cultures of Arizona and the Southwest.

The Luiseño boy's initiation ceremony was a long and especially dramatic affair. Tribal leaders had each initiate purify himself, drink the hallucinogenic drug *toloache* (Datura), and then dance until unconscious. This often produced a colorful, mystical vision. In the weeks of heightened sensitivity that followed, elders imparted songs, dances, and sacred knowledge. A sand painting, representing the entire cosmos, was made on the ground. Here, laid before the initiates's eyes, was a symbolic universe that consisted of astronomical and spiritual phenomena interspersed with "avengers" such as bear-cougar and raven. As the youths studied the sand painting, an older man explained its meaning.

See these [sand painting figures], these are alive, this is bear-cougar; these are going to catch you if you are not good and do not respect your elder relatives and grown-up people. And if you do not believe, these are going to kill you; but if you do believe, everybody is going to see your goodness and you then will kill bear-cougar. And you will gain fame and be praised, and your name will be heard everywhere.

See this, this is the raven, who will shoot you with bow and arrow if you do not put out your winnowing basket. Harken, do not be a dissembler, do not be heedless, do not eat food of overnight [do not secretly eat food left after the last meal of the day]. Also you will not get angry when you eat, nor must you be angry with your elder relations.

The earth hears you, the sky and wood mountain see you. If you will believe this you will grow old. And you will see your sons and daughters, and you will counsel them in this manner, when you reach your old age. And if when hunting you should kill a hare or rabbit or deer, and an old man should ask you for it, you will hand it to him at once. Do not be angry when you give it, and do not throw it to him. And when he goes home he will praise you, and you will kill many, and you will be able to shoot straight with the bow....

Heed this speech and you will grow old. And they will say of you: "He grew old because he heeded what he was told." And when you die you will be spoken of as those of the sky, like the stars. Those it is said were people, who went to the sky and escaped death. And like those will rise your soul.   LUISEÑO

Initiation into the Ghost Society

A major event in a boy's life was his initiation into a secret society. Such societies flourished in north-central California, preserving sacred knowledge, ritual, songs, and dances, and passing them on to a younger generation. The Ghost Society, widespread among many different tribal groups, was apparently of ancient origin. Ghost Society members impersonated the spirits of the dead—a dangerous and fearful undertaking—and cured illnesses caused by ghosts. Their dance costumes consisted of long black poles, elaborate featherwork, and bodies painted with black, red, and white stripes. Such spectacular regalia combined life images with death images, thereby symbolizing the society's position as mediator between the world of the living and the world of the dead. By sponsoring initiation rites, the Ghost Society also mediated between the world of childhood and that of adulthood. A Yuki man, looking back upon his youth, recalls his initiation into the Ghost Society—although he is careful, of course, not to divulge any of the sacred knowledge that his grandfathers gave him at the time.

For the Ghost-Society Initiation everyone moved to the village of Ushichma'lha't, and the same day a dance house was put up. The logs were cut and everybody helped in their erection. That night the old men discussed among themselves how they could best catch me the next day.

In the morning they went out to cut the large center post and took me along. They found a good white oak in the canyon and cut its roots. They had no steel axes and worked with a large stone. When they were about to fell the tree itself they ordered me up into it. I was to sit on the crotch with my arms folded. They wanted to test me and see if I was a man and make me into someone who would be a chief. But they made the tree fall as lightly as they could so as not to hurt me. Then they chopped off the top above the fork in which I still sat. Now one of my uncles took off my boy's fawnskin and gave me a man's deerskin to wear. Then they took the log away. I lay flat on it. Thus they brought it into the dance house. They set it up in its hole and still I kept my place. Then my maternal grandfather reached up and took me off, laid me on his lap and cried over me. Then I could not help but cry too.

21

When the sun went down, they built a large fire and sweated themselves, but did not trouble me. For four days I was in the dance house with many other boys, all of us eating nothing. My maternal grandfather, and also my paternal grandfather, Lamsch'ala, talked to me about the Ghost Society.

This was late in the fall, when the river first began to rise. After four days I was allowed to eat and drink again, but all winter they kept me hidden away in the dance house. Whenever I went outdoors my face was covered. All through the winter at intervals they had the Ghost Society performance for four days at a time. They made it for themselves, not to teach me. But my grandfathers told me to watch them and to see everything that they did. Between times they kept me well covered up. Every evening they sweated. Thus they did until late spring when the grass seeds were ripe.

The second time I went through the Initiation was at Suk'a. I was a big boy now. This time the ceremonies lasted only four days. After the meal at the end I belonged to the dance house [as a full initiate] and went with the others to bring wood for sweating. Between the first ceremony and this one my grandfathers had taught me fully all the songs that I must know.

The third time I took part I was a grown and married man. Now I took part in the building of the dance house and all the other work. I danced and helped to give orders. I was practicing to be an important man. YUKI

The first Ghost-Society-Initiation lasted from the time "when the river first began to rise" until the time "when the grass seeds were ripe"— from early December until May or June, a six month period during which the youth kept to the dance house and devoted himself exclusively to religious instruction. No one considered this excessive. Throughout life a proper person would put large amounts of time aside for dancing, singing, praying, fasting, and other ritual observances. For Indian people everywhere in California, such activities were as fully necessary for human life as the hunting of game or the gathering of acorns.

II: The Conflict of Love

I am a fine-looking woman;
Still, I am running with my tears.

Maidu song

How the Woman Got Even

When it came time to marry, the prospective groom approached his family to give or lend him the "bride-price"—gift baskets, money beads, skins, featherwork, and other treasure objects that he would have to pay to the bride's family. If his relatives were poor, he might (among some groups) be allowed to perform labor for the bride's family in lieu of material payment.

Bride-price was an honored custom almost everywhere in California, absent only at the fringes of the state—east of the Sierra and along the Colorado River. Among some groups, such as the Yokuts, it had become reduced to a gesture—a symbolic gift passed from the groom's family to the bride's family to legitimize the union. In northwestern California, however, bride-price was extraordinarily important. Among the Hupa, for instance, a woman's status was judged entirely by the bride-price she had fetched. So was her children's status. If a man's mother had gotten a huge bride-price he would be highly esteemed and assumed to be of noble character and unassailable integrity. Throughout his life people would treat him with honor and respect. A man whose mother had received only a small bride-price was considered ill-bred and was constantly suspected of lying and cheating. As for a man whose mother had received no bride-price at all, he was called *tintailtcwen,* "born-in-the woods." Such a man was a social outcast, generally a slave. He was never allowed to set foot in the sacred sweat-house. If he ever married it was only to someone of the same caste. If he was killed, no money could be exacted from his murderer. Throughout his life he would be addressed in terms generally used for dogs.

Along with the strong emphasis on bride-price, the northwestern California people tended to have austere attitudes toward sex. Men slept separately from women, and innumerable restrictions and taboos discouraged too frequent love-making. In fact among the Hupa the taboos were so prevalent that almost all sexual contact was said to have taken place in late summer and early fall when people left their villages (and ordinary lives) to camp in the hills. Almost all Hupa babies were born in the late spring.

A similar austerity prevailed among the Hupa's neighbors, the Karok. For the Karok, as for the Hupa, marriage was basically a financial

25

transaction rather than a romantic fulfillment. The woman whom the Karok held out as an ideal was the one who got—not the man she *loved*— but rather the highest possible bride-price.

A woman was walking upslope to Ipputtatc; she was going for wood, and she was packing along fire at the same time. Then all at once she saw somebody downriver coming in the upslope direction. He stopped; he looked. He was carrying his quiver, holding it high up. He said: "What are you packing fire for?" She answered: "I am cold." "What, the quail is already hollering, and nobody is carrying fire; nobody will feel cold," he said laughing. "I am going to Amekyaram. They are catching salmon already at Amekyaram." He was laughing, he was just laughing; he was making fun of her packing fire. Then he went on upriver. The woman too went on upslope. She was going to get wood. After walking a little way, she looked up in the air. "Behold it is going to rain. It is all clouded over." Then she thought: "Oh, I wish it would rain; oh, I wish it would snow." Then she prepared the wood, chipping off dry fir bark with a wedge. After a while it was snowing, dry snow; it was snowing a big fall of dry snow. The girl made a big fire there, where she was getting the wood ready. Then she thought: "Just a little later now and I will go downslope." All she could think about was that man. She was mad at him because, "Why did he laugh at me? That fellow said: 'I will be passing through here on my way back this evening, at sundown.'" She thought: "I guess he is about coming back." Then she put the load on her back. The snow was up to her ankles. She was walking along. She carried the fire back again as she went downslope; she was carrying it in her bowl basket, and she had the wood, too, on her back.

Then all at once there was a noise behind her. It was the man who hollered: "Stop, I want to talk with you." She stopped.

He said: "Do something good for me; make a fire for me. I am cold." The woman laughed. Then she said: "The quail is hollering; nobody ever feels cold. Nobody feels cold. You are not cold, I think you are telling a story." "Make a fire for me. I am carrying here in my hand a head-cut of salmon. Make me a fire for that. I am carrying here in my hand a head-cut of salmon." "No!" "I have here a pair of hair club bands with woodpecker scalps on them." Then she said: "No!" "Well then, I will give you my quiver, and all that is inside of it; all that I will give you." "No!" "I will give you my fishery, Ickecatcip." "No!" "I am carrying inside here a flint knife." "No!" "Well then, my armor; I will give you my armor." "No!" "Well then, let me marry you then; you can make a slave out of me." "Well then, I will make a fire." So she made a fire, a fire. The man warmed himself. Then he was all right; he warmed himself thoroughly.

Then they went home, to Xavnamnihitc, to the woman's house. She had him for her slave, and they were going to live at her house [not the man's house, the more usual marital arrangement]. She was happy, she was laughing all the time. That is what Xavnamnihitc-woman did. KAROK

Thus Xavnamnihitc-woman got a fine bride-price—not only treasure, but ownership of the man himself. No wonder she was laughing! She was the idealized Karok heroine: calculating, firmly insistent that her rights be respected, quick to take advantage of a situation, and *always* attentive to wealth and material possessions.

Although the Karok and their neighbors emphasized bride-price far more than did other California Indians, their attitudes were not so much an exception as an extreme development of attitudes common throughout much of the state. Why was bride-price so important? Perhaps because (despite the story of Xavnamnihitc-woman) it generally gave family control over the marriage. The groom, scarcely more than a youngster, would not have acquired sufficient treasure to legitimize his marriage, and the penalties for marrying without bride-price were too severe to be borne. Thus the groom would have to go to his family, which would thereby have power over whom the son would marry. Similarly, by accepting or rejecting the offer, the bride's family had control over their daughter. Indeed, throughout California marriages were generally arranged by the family. Love—the passionate desire of one individual for another—was not held to be a necessary foundation for a successful marriage. The honor and economic advantage of the family was the foremost concern, the passion of the individual (as always) was secondary.

27

Three Love Songs

Despite the austerity of people in northwestern California, despite the prevalence of arranged marriages everywhere, and despite the many restrictions on sex, love still raged beneath the surface—as poignant, pressing, and irreducibly tender as it is throughout the world.

I.

Before you go over the snow-mountain to the north,
Downhill toward the north,
Oh me, do look back at me.

You who dwell below the snow-mountain,
Do look back at me.

II.

When he walks about,
When he walks about,
Pushing the deer decoy back away from his face,
Right there in front of him
May I come gliding down and fall!

III.

The sleeping place
Which you and I hollowed out
Will remain always,
Will remain always,
Will remain always,
Will remain always.   WINTU

The Handsome Man

Amidst the restrictions and family pressures, people gave themselves over to love—sometimes tragically, sometimes foolishly, sometimes comically, often hopelessly. And they gave themselves over to love stories, too—stories that explored love in all its pleasant and its painful aspects. The Wintu called love stories "Nini," because they were ritually preceded and followed by the refrain, *hinini,* repeated again and again.

T here was a couple who had one son. The little boy grew up and became handsome. No one ever saw him. The people talked among themselves. "They say he is a handsome man," they said. Women from all over heard about him. They came in numbers to where the man dwelt, and surely it was because they wanted to see him. The women who came lived in houses nearby. They watched, but they did not see him.

Now at daybreak that man used to go bathing in the creek, but no one saw him. So the women who had come watched three and many days for him, yet they did not see him. Other women came from the west and from the north. They continued to come, and new ones arrived, and they all talked among themselves. The man heard them. He disliked all the women, so he did not want to stay.

Now all the women went to bathe where the man was accustomed to bathe. They saw damp tracks on the ground, and in the water they found a long hair. When they found the hair they all rushed to get it. Once they had seen the hair, they all wanted to see the man, saying, "It must have fallen from his head." So they thought, "Let's watch tomorrow."

The man, disliking them all, spoke to his father and mother, saying, "I am not going to stay here."

The next morning the women went to bathe, planning to catch a glimpse of the man; but the man had gone to bathe before them. So when the women went downhill to the creek there were already damp tracks returning. They were all very much annoyed.

In the evening the women lay talking to one another. "Let us watch this evening," they said. So early in the evening they went along the trail to the creek. Two went south and sat along the creek. A little further up, west of the trail, two more sat. But the man knew already that they were to watch for him. Now the women sat watching all night. They sat, and sat, and sat, all of them. And the dawn came, and they slept sitting as they were. When they were asleep for a short while, the man went to the water, bathed, and after bathing came back to his house. Then the women woke up, went down to the water, and behold! there were wet tracks already returning. They were all annoyed, and talked together. They almost wept.

The man, after he got home, warmed himself by the fire, and after warming himself he parted his hair and spread it out. After a time it dried and the old woman got the meal ready. When he had eaten, he spoke. "I will go away this morning," he said to his parents. So after he had finished eating and had combed his hair, he got some red rock powder and some tail fat and mixed them together. Then he painted himself and took his weapons and said, "Well, I'm going." And they said, "Yes," to their son. He then went outside and stood in front of his house, and the women now saw him.

Among the women were two sisters who had wanted terribly to see him, and they too saw him. So the man stood around, wishing that all should see him. Then he went off toward the west. The two sisters went into the house, got their carrying baskets, and followed after him, running. They went at a running pace over North Flat, wishing to see the man who had gone before them. The man was not to be seen, but there lay his tracks going forward. And they ran, they went at a running pace; they went rapidly. At South-Slope-Climb they looked northward, but did not see him. "We'll see him going uphill at Waitisawi," they thought to themselves. But they did not see him; he had already gone by.

The women went on running. They came to the ridge north of Dula and looked across the canyon, saying, "He'll be going that way." Still they did not see him. "*Hala,* he must be hurrying terribly much," they said.

So they ran, they went at a running pace across the canyon and up Nosono, and then they came to a stop. Looking down on the ground, behold! there were tracks going eastward. When they saw the tracks they ran toward the east until they came in sight of Rock-House-Lowland-Walk. There was a creek with running water. And when they looked, behold! that was where the man had stopped to drink, dipping water up in wild rhubarb leaves, and leaving the rhubarb leaves behind. Behold! there were damp tracks, he had just gone by that way. They pounced on the rhubarb leaves. Each girl pressed the rhubarb leaves against her heart, put them against her body here and there, because the man had held them in his hands.

Then they went on; they went running, running up the hill. When they reached the top they could look far ahead, but they could not see him. They kept on going at a running pace, and when they reached the top they looked to the north. They still did not see him. So they went on running; they kept on going at a rapid pace, and they arrived in sight of Digger-Pine-Broken-Off-In-Front. And behold! to the north they saw the man sitting, sitting with his face to the east. And they ran fast, keeping their eyes on him. One sat down on one side of him, the other sat down on his other side. Then they put their arms around him, and both said, "Why did you hurry so?" The man said, "I did not hurry." "We came at a rapid pace, so you must have run," they said. And he said, "No, I didn't." And they both sat there.

Then the man said, "I thirst for water. Do go and bring water, you two." "Where may the water be?" they asked. "Down the hill to the north, there is water in West Creek," he said. And they said, "You are finding an excuse because you want to go and leave us." "I won't," he said: "no, one of you two go and bring the water." However, they did not want to go and bring water. Then one said, "Younger sister, you had better go and bring water." Still they were unwilling to go, grudging each other the man. Then the man said to them, "I am thirsty. Hurry and get me water, you two, then we can start on our way." Still they did not want to go. Then he said, "Both of you go. I'll wait for you." Finally they said, "We'd better go. Don't leave us." And he said, "I won't."

They took out the drinking baskets that they had brought with them and went. They went running. They went running down the hill to the creek, and when they got there, they sipped water; they dipped up water and drank it. Then they dipped up another cupful and brought it running to where the man had sat. But when they reached the place, behold! the man was not there. Then they said to each other, "You were the one who wanted to go," they said. And the women threw themselves on the ground and wept, and after a while they saw smoke in the east. They waited, and soon they saw smoke even further toward the east. And they wept. "We won't go," they said. They lay there and lay there until afternoon. "We won't go," they said. Finally they sat up. Then they sang.

> Ni, ni, ni, ni, ni, ni,
> East and north from Skunk Mountain.
> Lutustini's child,
> Lutustini's child,
> Goes east and north.
> Along his going
> Smoke rises.
> It hangs over the south.
> Lutustini's child
> Goes east and north.
> Ni, ni, ni, ni, ni.

Then they went home, they went home crying.   WINTU

Football Free-for-All

People throughout California certainly fell in love. Even in the puritanical northwestern part of the state, tender stories were told of poor young men who by magic and hard work accumulated enough of a bride-price to marry the women they loved. Also, most groups in varying degrees were tolerant of premarital sex, homosexuality, certain cases of infidelity, polygamy, divorce, and remarriage. People of all ages relished sexual jokes and delighted in the raunchiest of Coyote stories. Among many groups there were certain seasons and certain ceremonies during which sexual looseness was not only permitted but even encouraged.

Sometimes a football game was called, the women playing the men, putting up valuables and even money to bet with each other. The men kicked the ball with the foot while the women caught it with the hand and ran with it. The men hugged the woman who carried the ball. When they tickled her belly, she threw the ball to another woman.

If that woman missed, a man kicked the ball with the foot. Another woman caught it with the hands and ran with it towards their goal. Then a man hugged her again. When he threw her on the ground and rolled her around, she threw the ball. In that way another woman caught it and brought it towards their goal.

The men played with the foot, the women played with the hand: that was their playing together so that a man could hug the woman he loved. The women on their part took every opportunity to hug the men they loved; the game was like that so that this could be done.

NISENAN

Tolowim-Woman and Butterfly Man

Native Californians had paradoxical and complex attitudes toward sex. On one hand people fell in love and had wide sexual experiences. On the other hand, sex was seen as threatening, dangerous, inimical to spiritual pursuits. People about to hunt, gamble, dance, seek power, collect medicine, or engage in any serious venture were warned to avoid love-making. Against the passion of the individual, the voice of society repeated its message: be prudent, moderate, obedient, restrained. Yet how difficult it was to heed that message! A woman gathering food in a meadow might stop now and then to indulge in a fantasy. How wonderful it would be, she might daydream, if an irresistible lover were suddenly to appear.

A Tolowim-woman went out to gather food. She had her child with her; and while she gathered the food, she stuck the point of the cradle-board in the ground, and left the child thus alone. As she was busy, a large butterfly flew past. The woman said to the child, "You stay here while I go and catch the

33

butterfly." She ran after it, and chased it for a long time. She would almost catch it, and then just miss it. She wore a deer-skin robe. She thought, "Perhaps the reason why I cannot catch the butterfly is because I have this on." So she threw it away. Still she could not catch the butterfly, and finally threw away her apron and hurried on. She had forgotten all about her child, and kept on chasing the butterfly till night came. Then she lay down under a tree and went to sleep.

When she awoke in the morning, she found a man lying beside her. He said, "You have followed me thus far, perhaps you would like to follow me always. If you would, you must pass through a lot of my people." All this time the child was where the woman had left it, and she had not thought of it at all. She got up, and followed the butterfly-man. By and by they came to a large valley, the southern side of which was full of butterflies. When the two travellers reached the edge of the valley, the man said, "No one has ever got through this valley. People die before they get through. Don't lose sight of me. Follow me closely."

They started and travelled for a long time. The butterfly-man said, "Keep tight hold of me, don't let go." When they had got halfway through, other butterflies came flying about in great numbers. They flew every way, about their heads, and in their faces. They were fine fellows, and wanted to get the Tolowim-woman for themselves. She saw them, watched them for a long time, and finally let go of her husband, and tried to seize one of these others. She missed him, and ran after him. There were thousands of others floating about; and she tried to seize, now one, now the other, but always failed, and so was lost in the valley.

She said, "When people speak of the olden times by and by, people will say that this woman lost her lover, and tried to get others but lost them, and went crazy and died." She went on then, and died before she got out of the valley. The butterfly-man she had lost went on, got through the valley, and came to his home.

MAIDU

To desert child and family and run with complete abandon after love and beauty—this is indeed at the heart of many a daydream. But as the fate of the Tolowim-woman poignantly suggests, destruction awaits those

34

who seek freedom and unrestrained joy. The moral is clear: freedom leads to ruination and one had best follow the middle way—the way of moderation and restraint, the way of the family.

Women are Troublemakers

Perhaps because marriages were often arranged by family, and perhaps because of the sense that love-making was harmful to spiritual and other valued activities, the relationship between husband and wife tended to be somewhat aloof. The woman associated with other women throughout the day, making baskets, grinding acorns, collecting roots and berries. The man kept company with other men—in some tribal groups even living together in the sweat-house apart from the women and children. Marriage did not seem to be the most important relationship in one's life, and generally a person had closer ties to natal family than to a spouse.

Women are troublemakers: an old woman said that to me when I was young. Out of my four women, only one got along with me nicely. Indian women are jealous. Children will get you into trouble. The older people teach us not to get in the habit of fussing with our wives, and if one starts complaining, to walk away if you can. A woman is more jealous than a man. A man isn't after a woman for nothing.

As a rule, a poor man has more children, but I guess he lies around and has more babies. A man of importance isn't around the house very much. Such a person hardly ever jokes with his wife. He may only be around in the evening. He may lie down alone for a while and then come to her to get warm. There are some men who like to be around their women all the time. They get to hating each other bitterly after a little while....

A couple can decide to separate by agreement. If a woman who is a basketmaker wants to leave a man, she will make him a real nice basket, mad and pouting all the time. This may take her from six months to a year. She will remain there and work for him and talk to him, but the two will simply not be getting along very well. When she finishes the basket she will hand it to him, saying that she is leaving. He gives it to his mother and tells her what has happened. Now the man's parents have to give her parents something. That is a friendly separation. NOMLAKI

The marriage might break up, but as always the deep, organic relationship between children and parents survives.

III: An Ordered World

The young chief is going to do the same
*   as his father used to do.*
Now all of you men get ready.
Put those poles up for him.
All of you men get ready.
Have the ceremonial house ready just
*   the same as for his father.*
The young chief is going to do just the
*   same as his father.*
He is going the same way as his father did.
It is just the same, just the same.

Speech upon inaugurating a new chief,
Miwok

Tarantula

A couple began their married life together in a world where custom determined one's behavior. There was a correct way of doing everything—collecting shellfish, making baskets, building a house—and to deviate from the accepted ways was unthinkable and ridiculous. Only a complete idiot would try to do things differently. Among the Coast Yuki a man named Tarantula was such an idiot.

T here was a man named Tarantula. He had a wife. Tarantula did not know much. His wife had to tell him everything. They lived, lived together, all right.

Once Tarantula went to the beach at Mussel Rock [*Lilem*]. He was going to make himself a basket. He did not break up the hazel brush like anyone else; instead he bunched it as it stood growing. He made a basket, working around and around, until it was very big and high. When he finished with that, he collected mussels and filled the basket with them. Then he attached a pack strap, so he could carry it. He got under the basket and tried to lift, but could not, because it was fastened by the roots. He tramped around and strained and made a large hole where he was trying to get it up.

After a while his wife found him. She looked for him, because she did not know what had become of him.

She said: "My goodness, you crazy thing. You don't know anything. You ought to die!"

She transferred the mussels to another basket and took them and him home. They built a dwelling house. They got redwood bark for the sides. They kept at it until it was finished. She told him: "When you finish the house put earth around the bottom." He went out and threw up earth. He kept throwing up earth, until it was all covered like an assembly house. She went out to see what he was doing. There he was throwing up earth as fast as he could.

"You crazy thing, what is the matter with you?" she asked. "You ought to go off and die; you don't know anything." They finished the house. Everything was done.

After completing the house, Tarantula went after more mussels. She said: "Now, you get hazel twigs, break them off and make a basket. Don't make a basket growing." "Hech," Tarantula said. Then he went to Mussel Rock. He made a basket, kept working, working until he could no longer reach; then he quit. He broke off the twigs this time. He got mussels and started back. He did not return by the trail, but went under the ground like a gopher.

His wife was sitting on the ground in their house. She felt something moving the ground, like a gopher. She got up and looked and got ready with a pestle to strike the gopher when it came up. The ground kept moving, moving. She stood with pestle poised to strike.

Pretty soon Tarantula's head appeared. "You crazy thing, you ought to go off and die," she said. "You don't know anything, you crazy thing. People who go to get mussels should come by the trail." Then Tarantula went back into the ground. He went out of his tunnel at its starting point; then came up the trail.

When he returned by the trail, he did not put his basket down when he arrived, but stood with it on his back. She went out of the house and found him standing there with the basket on his back. He had not taken it off yet.

She said: "When people come up the trail with mussels or anything they should lay their basket down, then go inside and sit down." He went in and sat down; never moved, just sat there. He sat there.

"My goodness," she said, "when people come up the trail with mussels or anything and sit down, they should move around a little and eat." She fixed food and he ate. He kept eating, would not stop. She said: "Some time, when you get enough, stop for a while. Sometimes men and women play together." "Hech," he replied. He played with her, squeezed and hugged her; they played like two children. Pretty soon, she got tired. "Oh my goodness," she said, "sometimes they have to quit playing." "Hech," he said. He quit. The woman said: "Sometimes they sit down and talk." "Hech," he said. He sat there saying nothing; sat there as though he were dead, did not look around, did not say a word. "My goodness," she said, "sometimes people lie down."

He lay down; lay there, lay there, lay there. "Oh," she said, "sometimes people pack wood and make a fire."

He went out and got wood, packed wood, and packed wood, without stopping. Finally, she made him stop.

One day it was raining. The house was leaking. She said: "You'd better go out and find some redwood bark to stop this leak." He went on top of the house and lay his body over the leaky place, instead of getting bark. He lay there a long time and his wife did not know what had become of him. He almost died of the cold, as he lay there wet and shivering.

"I'd like to know what's the matter with you," she said. "You ought to go off and die. You don't know anything, you crazy thing."

COAST YUKI

The Osegen Slave at Espeu

Yurok villages dotted the mouth of the Klamath River and the coast near-by. The Yurok had not always lived there. In ancient times they must have migrated from the east, for their language is distantly related to the Algonkin languages of eastern North America. But all records of that migration was lost long ago, even to myth, and in the Yurok vision of the world, Yurok had been set down at the mouth of the Klamath at the very creation of the human race. Deeply rooted, they knew their land with profound intimacy. Large trees, clumps of bushes, even modest-size river rocks had proper names and stories. Villages like Osegen and Espeu—clusters of large, redwood-plank, pitched-roof houses—were viewed as ancient features; once established they were like rivers and mountains in their apparent permanence, and such villages had hundreds of stories and associations attached to them. Individual houses—or rather the house sites they were resting on—also had ancient names and histories. For a Yurok to say, "My father is from the house named *wogwu*, my mother from the house *sohtsu*," (as the narrator of the following account once described himself) was to communicate something rich in meaning and connotation, rich in history and myth. A person who was born on a prestigious house site, it was felt, had absorbed the power and history

41

which the house site had collected from previous generations. The Yurok inhabited an old, well-established, deeply-experienced world in which the interactions between families had been regulated for centuries by a complex, sophisticated legal system of liabilities and penalties—a legal system serviced by professional mediators who were paid for their judicial roles.

A young man from Espeu had been visiting at Welkwau. On his way back they asked him at Osegen to stay overnight, for it was getting late. In the morning three brothers at Osegen went to hunt sea lions on a rock about three-fourths of a mile opposite Emets Beach. They did not invite the young man from Espeu, but he went along. From on top of the rock they saw a squall off Rekwoi. They started home at once, but the squall caught them and the Espeu young man was drowned on the beach. Espeu talked of destroying Osegen, so Osegen offered to settle. They claimed that they had not invited him, but a Turip woman there said they had asked him to stay overnight. Anyway, even if he had been all alone and had lost his life on their beach, Osegen would have been liable. Nevertheless, it was a close case, and Espeu knew they could not exact too much, so they insisted merely on getting a slave, and did get him. He was the youngest brother of the three who had taken the dead man out.

So the slave stayed a long time. He had gone as a young man and was elderly now. His master let him go overnight to his old home sometimes. Then he began to stay longer, and finally he did not come back.

Then his owner, with his two sisters, came after him to Osegen and found him on the beach, surf fishing, with his relatives the Osegen people. The Espeu man promptly claimed him. Then the slave's nephew said that he was not going back any more. The Espeu man said that he would take him right then and there. Thereupon the Osegen man shot him with three arrows. His sisters tried to protect him, but it was too late. One of them did break the bow that shot the third arrow.

Then the older sister stayed with the body, while the other one ran home and summoned help to bring the dead man back. Besides his two sisters, who were unmarried, the dead man had two brothers and a son. They did not try to fight until after the burial.

Meanwhile the Osegen people talked it over and said they must make a settlement as soon as possible. They asked a man from a Big Lagoon village to come at once and act as their go-between. So on the seventh day three men from Big Lagoon went to Espeu. They had a smoke and then reported to Espeu that Osegen wanted to settle. The next day they brought the pay that was proffered: a red obsidian, a woodpecker headband, four strings of large dentalium money, two otterskins, and a large deerskin blanket.

But Espeu had already said the day before that they would not take any property; they wanted the killer's sister. They were meeting halfway between Espeu and Osegen, so that the go-betweens would not have to walk so far. For a day they argued with Osegen, but the man who had done the killing did not want to let his sister go. His relatives kept urging him, and after two days he finally said, "I will give her if Espeu lets the slave go free." So the girl from Osegen was married to the son of the man who had been killed.   YUROK

From a Yurok point of view, the story of the Osegen slave had a happy ending. The settlement was to the advantage of the murdered man's son, who acquired a wife without having to pay the steep bride-price that would ordinarily have preceded such a marriage. As for the woman, she would have been considered properly married and her children would have been considered legitimate—very important in the Yurok world. In fact she would have been very well thought of by everyone, since her bride-price had been established as more than "a red obsidian, a woodpecker headband, four strings of dentalium money, two otter skins, and a large deerskin blanket," a rather significant amount of treasure. Everyone, in short, made out well, and the account of the Osegen slave— with its careful attention to the details of negotiation—would have been preserved as a legal "case" to be used as precedent for the resolution of similar conflicts in the future.

Slavery, it might be pointed out, was not primarily an economic institution among the Yurok. A slave may have fetched firewood, hauled animal carcasses, and done other chores; but the family that owned a slave was not overly interested in exploiting the slave's labor. Rather it held the slave mostly to exalt its own status—and perhaps to socially humiliate the family of the slave. Indeed, the word *slave*—with all the connotations and images it invokes in the modern mind—should probably not be used to describe this relationship; but since we have no equivalent institution, the English language has no really suitable word.

Wealth—the great obsession of northwestern Californians—also had a rather different meaning. Almost never did a person use wealth to buy food, clothing, or other necessities. In fact acorns, salmon, and other basic needs were not for sale. Thus wealth was not really something to be spent, but rather to be conserved within a family, for it was wealth alone that conferred status. The more treasure one had, the greater one's social prestige. Wealth was also proof and measure of virtue. The phrases "a good person" and "a wealthy person" were completely synonymous and interchangeable in the Yurok mind. And for good reason. In this extremely litigious society anyone who was not virtuous—who transgressed in any manner upon others—would be sued and fined, and would ultimately lose wealth. Thus the accumulation of wealth—far from being socially destructive—was a sure sign that one was constantly and unfailingly devoted to socially approved behavior.

Property

The Nomlaki lived along the Sacramento River and in the hills to the west, in what are now Glenn and Tehama Counties. The Hill Nomlaki differed culturally from the River Nomlaki, and they were further subdivided into a number of distinct dialect groups. Political units consisted of tiny, independent village-states, each with a population of no more than twenty-five to 200 people.

Like most Native Californians, the Nomlaki were hunter-gatherers. Each fall people heaved carrying nets and burden baskets onto their shoulders and left the major villages to gather acorns in the hills. They made similar treks for greens, roots, elk, salmon, and other commodities, often staying away from the major villages for weeks at a time as they ranged over their land.

The lack of large political units and the wandering style of life might lead one to think that the Nomlaki—who were fairly typical of Central California people—lived with a looseness of organization that bordered on anarchy. Yet the impression is false. The wanderings followed a distinct yearly pattern, and—as the following reminiscence indicates—the landscape over which people "wandered" was far from a trackless wilderness.

The land does not belong to individuals. Dominic's grandfather [a chief], by being such a big and good man, was favored. He was left a big valley. He owned one big oak tree of a special kind. It was a singular tree called *nuis*. There was a village nearby, but old Dominic's grandfather owned that tree and got all the acorns from it. He also owned a valley of about 2,000 acres of open land. It was two or three miles away from his home. This valley was staked off—each different division [kin group] got a different part of the valley for themselves. They had poles to mark the different persons' territories....

Where there is a tree of small acorns, some family owns that tree. He [the family head] will lean a stick against the tree on the side toward which he lives. Thus the people know what family owns it. He may set up too many and will give away the others to his relatives. This person kind of owns the tree—like you would a fruit tree. In those days the families owned them. They own trees in the mountains, too. They maintain border lines, but if you are friendly with them they may give you a tree in time of need.

NOMLAKI

Choosing a Chief

Within each tribal group there was generally a man of pre-eminence—a man who would in later years be variously called chief, headman, captain, or simply "the big man."

You know how some men are quick and strong and know the things to do, how people like to do things for them, and how they have a gift for getting everybody cheerful? Well, those men were leaders (*kwoxot*). When a man knew he had the power to be a good leader, he told his dreams. If his dreams were good, his plans would be followed, but if they were poor and stupid others would tell him so and he could do nothing. Sometimes men struggled with each other to lead war parties and arrange daily affairs. Then each would try to get more of the people on his side, giving feasts to his friends and encouraging them to speak of his wisdom. But it was not long before we knew who was the better man and he became leader and gave positions to others. If a leader acted stupidly, it meant that his power had deserted him and it was time to have another to decide things. A man did not become *kwoxot* because his father had been *kwoxot*, although some families were more powerful than others and had a lot of good men.

Kwoxot had to feed and look after poor people. He had to get together a big store of food for this. His followers gave him what they could spare, but this was not for his use, only for him to give away to the needy. When there was a death, the family burned its house and almost everything it had. Then they were very poor, without shelter and short of food, but they could go to the *kwoxot* and he would look after them; give them a place to live and food to eat. The *kwoxot* always did this for he was supposed to be kind to everyone, especially to widows. If he needed food for these people, he called on his followers and each gave a share of their stores....

Kwoxot had little to do with arranging ceremonies, he just did his part like anyone else. But he made the best speeches at these times. For it was by his speeches that people knew he had great power and was *kwoxot*.   Yuma

Throughout California chiefs had great prestige but little political power. They were not strong leaders, absolute monarchs, or despots in the tradition of other cultures. Far from it. They could persuade but could not give orders, for indeed they had no way of enforcing their decisions. People who did not like their ways generally ignored them. A chief who had lost the confidence of his people might harangue, lecture, or give advice, but people simply walked away. In societies where tradition and restraint were valued, where property and legal rights were deeply accepted, where warfare was limited, and where families were strong and autonomous units, a powerful chief was unnecessary and unwanted.

Early European explorers and commentators, who felt that a proper society required a strong ruler, looked upon Native Californians as living in anarchy. In reality political power was dispersed among family heads whose constant interactions, whose mutual respect for tradition, and whose checks and balances on each other made for a subtle, stable, and in many ways equitable form of government.

46

Messengers

There were over five hundred autonomous tribal groups in California—little nations, really—most of them numbering no more than a few hundred people. Each group tended to live in its own valley, more or less set apart from neighbors. Each group felt that it, and it alone, was the center of the world—the true "people" who did things the correct way. Others, they would insist (often quarrelsomely), had peculiar habits, spoke strange languages, did things all wrong. Each group was surrounded by "others" who were forever being suspected of treachery and evil magic.

Yet isolation between groups was far from complete. Despite the undercurrent of hostility and tension, each of these small tribal groups needed its neighbors for trade, for marriage partners, for ceremonies, or simply for entertainment. Life in these small, enclosed worlds could be somewhat boring, and a trip to a neighboring group—with different people, different land, games, dances, feasts, the telling of strange tales, and the sound of an alien tongue—was often the most exciting event of the year. After a long winter, when everyone had been kept home too long by rains and muddy trails, the urge to visit and socialize was especially strong.

Our people dance every spring and have all kinds of dances. When everything is all very green, when winter is over and everything is warm and the sun is coming north, when the birds holler *witwitwit*, the people begin to ask, "Why can't we play a little?" Then they send news to their close neighbors that they are going to have a dance....

The messenger who announces the *tami* [dance-feast] to neighboring villages and invites the people has strings with knots in them—one for each day until the dance is to start. One string is given to each headman of a village, and every day he unties one knot until they are all untied. The first knot is untied on the day that the messenger delivers it. The people come on the day the last knot is untied. The Indians used to laugh about this custom because now they can just say, "Next Saturday."

Newsboys [messengers] can carry news from Paskenta to Tehama and back between evening and dawn. It is about thirty miles each way. They trot. They have free passage into enemy territory. It is necessary that they eat special kinds of food which is

47

more preserving to the Indian body. The runners have to be careful of their diet. They are from twenty-five to forty years old, for they can't do this work when they are too young. They have to keep their wind. Special ones are picked for this—not just anyone. They try out on the plains—people say that that is the hardest place for runners.

The runner is in a dangerous position. He does no other work, for he must always be ready to go. When he isn't running, he practices. He doesn't hunt or fish, but is well taken care of....

Old blind Martin had been a newsboy. He made trips from Paskenta to Tehama. He said he never shot at a man in his life. He carried news over and back and had to remember every word he heard. After the runner comes back, after he catches his breath, he tells everything that was said. Two fellows repeat what he said, so that everything is heard three times. Everyone listens, and when they are all through they discuss the matter.   NOMLAKI

The messenger, as indicated, was chosen not only for his running ability, but for his good memory, for he had to keep even the most complicated and lengthy messages straight. Yet in these worlds that thrived before the introduction of writing, memory was highly developed. It has been noted that Native Californians who had heard an important speech just one time could repeat it twenty years later, the renditions of various listeners being almost identical.

Feast Oration

Feasts and dances allowed neighboring people to get together on a more or less formal and peaceful basis. Among the various Wintu tribal groups the Hesi dances were especially prominent. Hesi ceremonies were held twice yearly, in the fall and again in the spring, to insure plentiful harvests of acorns, greens, roots, seeds, and berries. They involved four full days of games, feasts, sweating, orations, dances, and other per-formances. The first day was devoted to preliminary dances. By the second day the sacred pole—twenty-five feet tall and "dressed" in feathers—was ushered out of the dance house and set into its proper place before the dance house entrance. Guests began arriving now, and the master of ceremonies came forth to give his welcoming speech. Because many of the guests were from other groups, there was a potential for trouble. Old grudges might flare up, new hostilities might be generated. The welcoming speech thus developed two major themes: "Enjoy yourselves," and "Don't quarrel." To prevent fights the master of ceremonies implores people to address each other by relationship words, to call each other "niece" and "nephew;" in short, to act like family.

The ritual context of the Hesi dance demanded a formal (rather than casual) welcoming speech—a speech in the full ceremonial manner. To California Indians speech-making was an art, as highly developed and in many ways as abstract as basketry, singing, or dancing. Indeed, speech-making was governed by a similar esthetic. Thus the Hesi welcoming speech is constructed much like a basket—winding around and around upon itself; creating, developing, and repeating patterns; weaving strong yet simple elements into an effective and urgent whole.

Yes!
Come on! Come on! Come on!
Come on!
Girls come on! Girls come on!
Youths come on!
Children come on!
At eating assembled. At eating assembled.
At this eating.
At this eating assembled.
At this *pinole* [seed-meal] assembled.
At this acorn-soup assembled.
At this acorn-bread assembled.
You say "yes" to one another!
Say "yes" to one another! Say "yes" to one another!
That is how you will do it!
You will call one another "nephew" or "niece."
At eating that.
At healthy eating assemble.
At eating that assemble. At eating this assemble.
At this pleasant eating assemble.
At this healthy eating assemble.
At that say "yes" to one another's eating!

Say "yes" to one another's eating!
Say "yes" to one another's eating!
Rejoice at one another.
Rejoice, "maternal uncle."
Rejoice, "father."
Rejoice, "younger brother."
Rejoice!
At him who causes you to eat.
At him who gives to you.
At him who gives food.
Who gives this *pinole*.
Who gives this acorn-bread.
At that be glad.
At that be glad.
So rejoice!
Rejoice for you.
My nephews and nieces, eat!
In this way eat! In this way eat! In this way eat!
You children.
You girls, you youths.
You children.
So eat!
So satisfied.
Satisfied, rejoice!
Satisfied, say "yes!"
Heed his word.
His word, his teaching.
He who teaches you.
So eat! So eat! So eat! So eat!   WINTU

Football Big-Time

Games provided another excuse for people to get together. Larger villages often had areas leveled and cleared for ball games, and each locality throughout the state had its own version of shinny or "soccer."

The Nisenan of the Sacramento Valley and Sierra Foothills favored a relay game in which each team tried to kick and carry its ball to a goal and back again to the starting point. The stakes were high (Native Californians loved to gamble) and the play was rough-and-tumble; nevertheless off the playing field restraint and ritual prevailed. Games were interspersed with ceremonial feasting, dancing, and socializing, and good form demanded that the losing team accept even the most crushing defeat with equanimity.

I n the early days the Indians had football "big-time." Very early in the morning the other team put up a great deal of money [i.e. many beads]. If they made goals at both ends of the field they won. Then they danced to make fun of us. When we finished we ate breakfast. After breakfast we played football again. At midday we rested, then we ate. When the sun came round to the west we were at it again; we only quit when the sun went down. We danced at night.

When it was dawn we played football again. We did that for two or three days and only quit when we had lost our money, valuables, baskets, clothes, bows. Before we parted we ate, the men of this side treating the other side. Then the men of the other side treated this side. Only then did we go each on his way. That was football "big time." NISENAN

Warfare

Many Native American groups outside California valued warfare: warrior cults and war chiefs played an important part in their tribal life; adolescent boys were expected to kill an enemy or "count coup" before attaining full manhood; bravery and war prowess were qualities for which every self-respecting man strove. By comparison, Native Californians were by and large peaceful—or at least they *valued* peace, even if they did not always attain it. The quarrelsomeness and suspicion between neighboring groups often led to skirmishes; yet war for its own sake was rarely practiced in California, except at the extreme edges of the state—among the Modoc of the Oregon border and among the Colorado River people. Most Californians saw warfare as an evil to be avoided; a "last resort;"

an unpleasant act into which "we"—a proper and innocent people—had been forced by the insolent and intolerable behavior of those "others" who lived beyond the next ridge.

I n war times there are arrow carriers, who also carry spears. Normally everyone carries his own, but in tight places they give the extra arrows to these carriers. There is always a lookout on watch when a group of women are gathering seeds. If anyone comes to molest the women, the lookout will yell a war whoop in warning, and the people know what that means. They know by the way the watcher yells that fighting or killing is going on.

People fight at close range. They let their fastest runner use the elkhide. He runs up close and then crouches down. The men come and stand behind this shield. The enemy can't hit the Huta [secret society] members because they dodge the arrows and are good fighters. If a warrior wastes his ten arrows without results, he doesn't fight any more. They never shoot back the enemies' arrows, but they might save them. A man who is being held at bay may shoot back an enemy arrow, however. They quit fighting just at sunset. The peacemaker will yell, "Quit, the sun is down."

It is against the rules to throw rocks at an enemy who is being held at bay hiding under a bush. They won't shoot arrows at such a person unless they actually see him. It is too wasteful of arrows.

They aren't allowed to club one another—they can spear, knife, or shoot. They carry the *sen* [a manzanita burl club], but aren't supposed to use it.

They never talk about wars except among themselves, and then only in a whisper. They don't brag about what they have done except at the place where they have killed the man.   NOMLAKI

Throughout California wars were fought, but they were waged with apparent reluctance—indeed, with the same restraint and adherence to tradition that characterized Native California life in general.

The Great Horned Owls

A well-regulated, peaceful, thoroughly domestic world: that is what
Native Californians valued most. Each person in this world was expected
to perform his or her role properly. The man of the family would hunt and
bring home plenty of meat. The wife would collect roots, seeds, and nuts,
cook, tend the house, and "keep her baskets right." The child, of course,
would obey. Many an exemplary tale extolled this ordered world and
warned of the terrible fate that would befall people who deviated from
their assigned roles.

A married couple and one child lived at a place called Mal-
kabel. They lived there a long time. They ate food, both
acorn mush and deer. The man was always going hunting;
he shot many deer at a time and laid them down at home—some he
dried. And from the coast, too, he used to gather mussels and aba-
lone, and these he frequently set down at home. The child used to
eat; it was a small child, about three or four years old.

Then, one time, he arrived carrying a deer. The mother got
everything ready; she cooked acorn mush and deer. "All right,
let's eat," she said. The man said, "OK." When the food was
ready, they took their mussel-shell spoons and ate the mush. After
serving her husband, the wife attended to the child.

She summoned the child. It didn't mind; it failed to heed her; it
just sat. "Come eat; you must be starved," said the mother. It
didn't obey; it just sat. Then after a while the woman said to her
husband, "Let's eat alone."

That man turned out not to be the father—he was the stepfather
of the child. Then they ate—they ate for a while. When they had
finished their food, they put the rest away. When they did so, the
child started to cry. It sat there crying for it hadn't eaten any food.
It cried and cried for a long time. Then the man said, "Apparently
the crying will never stop. If it keeps crying, I'll push it outside."

Then he arose. His wife tried to stop him, but he shoved her out
of the way. He then set the little child outside and tied the door fast
so that the mother couldn't pull it open. He held the mother in the

53

house. Because the mother wanted to open the door, the man held her in the house.

The child cried for a long time outside. "Let me in," it said while crying. Then suddenly Great Horned Owls hooted while flying along—two or three perhaps. They were getting closer and closer. Meanwhile the man was holding the mother to prevent her from opening the door. Suddenly the Great Horned Owls carried the child off. The mother heard the crying dying away into the distance.

Now the man went to sleep. The mother just sat there until dawn. When day broke the man arose and again went hunting. When he had gone the mother set out in the direction that she had heard the child's crying.

It turned out to be a long way from the house. She walked along. Suddenly, when she stopped to stand under a big tree, bones were lying under there. The mother gathered all of the bones into a burden basket. She was rushing before the man returned. She laid a fire and poured the bones onto it in order to burn them up. When the fire had burned them all to cinders, they became powder-like. Then, having filled a basket with that, she carried it home. Next she stirred up some acorn mush—a lot of mush. When the acorn mush was cooked, she sprinkled some of that powder into one basket and set it over in the rear of the house, but her own she kept apart.

In the evening, just as the sun was setting, the man arrived and set down a deer. "I'm hungry; is there any acorn mush?" he asked his wife. "Yes, there is some that I have set aside for you," she said. Then she placed the mush before him. When she did so, the man picked up a mussel shell and ate; he ate it all clean.

By that time it was already dark. He stretched himself out—the woman too—but when she lay down she couldn't sleep; she just stayed awake all night. Suddenly when it was approaching daylight, the man wanted to talk with his wife, but he couldn't utter a sound—only his mouth could move. Unexpectedly, after a little while, he died.

When the woman arose, she saw that he had died. He just lay there. Then, having prepared her food, she ate. When she had finished her acorn mush, she got all of her things ready—she filled a finely woven burden basket with her possessions, and with her child's possessions too. But her husband's belongings she just left lying there. When she was ready, she carried the burden basket outside and set it down off by itself.

Then she lay some dry grass against the house and set fire to it. The man was lying in there dead. The house blazed up and burned. When everything else was burned, the man, too, burned. Then the woman set out for another settlement—she packed her belongings along to where her relatives lived.

They asked, "What happened to the child?" She just cried at first. When she did so, the relatives knew what had happened. Then she told, "My child is dead. My husband pushed it outside and the Great Horned Owls carried it away and evidently ate it. When that happened, I burned the bones up, ground them, and sprinkled some on acorn mush. When he ate that mush, he died, and I burned the house and left."

"It is a good thing that you have done, for we would have killed him anyway," her brothers said.

Then she lived there—lived there for a long time. Her brothers fed her now. They lived there for generations.

This my grandmother told us, saying that this old time story was true. This is the end.   POMO

At the close of the story, the family is established once more; like a chorus it intones the verdict and restores a sense of wholeness to a deeply injured world. The theme is repeated yet again: people suffer and die, the family endures.

Building a Dance House

Life in many of the larger Central California villages centered around a communal building. Such buildings were huge—sometimes up to sixty feet in diameter. They were generally underground or partially underground, and a person passing down the sloping entranceway walked into a world of deep, earthen smells. The temperature was relatively constant throughout the year, the lighting always dim. During the day a narrow shaft of sunlight came through the smoke hole and swept slowly across the floor; a fire flickered at night, casting huge shadows upon the walls. In such dark, cavernous, mysterious places people gathered for ceremonies, public events, and sacred dances. These buildings were variously called "assembly houses," "earth lodges," "round houses," or "dance houses."

When they want to build a dance house, all the important men get together in the *elkel* [chief's house] and talk about where they can get the trees. They have all the posts and ribs of the structure named, and the men mention the various logs they have seen that would meet the needs of the different parts. They do not speak of their decision to anyone, but go out and look at the tree that is to form the center pole. They will walk around the tree and examine every detail of it.

Before any further steps are taken, the group goes to the captain of the village and asks his approval of their plan. He will not answer them for a long time, perhaps as much as an hour, and then he may ask them if they are in a position to build a *lut* [dance house]. They will tell him what food they have in store. He will ask, "How do your women feel?" and they will reply that it is all right with them. This procedure is necessary because it is expensive to build a dance house, as they must feed all the neighboring people who assist in the construction and are invited to the dance that follows. The headman can [theoretically] stop the building of a house. Others might object to it, but their only protest is to move to another village.

Having decided to build a house, the men begin to prepare the poles. These are cut down, trimmed, and barked, a fork being left at the top. The cutting of the poles may take a month. The one selected as the center pole is the last pole to be cut. Finally they select a place to dig the hole for the dwelling, and by this time the people have caught on to what is in the air without being told, and those who are next to the important men come to help.

The house is built in one day. The people have gathered and brought what food they could. They all get to work digging out the pit, each person working by digging with his *sen* [club] and carrying the earth out in the conical carrying baskets. Each works in that portion of the excavation toward which his own home lies. By working hard together, they finish the hole in three or four hours. Everyone helps, women, children, and men—all but the menstruant girls.

Then important men have meanwhile gone to the location of the center pole and have dressed it as a dancing man with a feather headdress. It is carried to the house pit by six or eight men on a "stretcher" made of grapevine, accompanied by two singers, who sing a "march." They do not set the pole down till they get to the hole, where they set it upright in a special way and tamp it into place.

Next they put the two "brothers" in place and then the other upright posts; then the ribs are put from ground to post and between posts, a man being ready at each joint to do the lashing. Then smaller sticks and finally wormwood are added, each person again working on that portion lying in the direction of his home. After the wormwood is laid over the ribs, the crannies are stuffed with moss, and earth is carried onto the roof and spread over it to a thickness of about three or four inches. It is packed down by constantly walking over it, so that in the end the house is nearly airtight except for the door and smoke hole. At the last the people from the several surrounding villages try to finish their side first, and this work is done in high spirits, the people teasing and making fun of one another. Those first finished raise a great shout and help the others to finish the work.

The house is completed by night, and after this there is either feasting or a "sweat" or both. The hosts are expected to feed their guests for some time, and usually their entire supply of food is exhausted by the occasion.

The dance house belongs to the dancing men and the people, but the chief bosses and uses it, and it is called his. He does not live in it, but has it merely as a meeting house. His own house is the smaller sweat-house called *elkel*.   NOMLAKI

The building of the dance house was a joyous, boisterous affair. Men, women, and children crowded onto the site and worked shoulder-to-shoulder, excavating the hole, raising the posts, lashing the beams, and piling the earth onto the roof. Afterwards they feasted and celebrated. What seeming chaos! Yet the confusion was only apparent, as the preceding account suggests. The entire enterprise was well-ordered and carefully planned with the debates and deliberations, the hierarchy of "important" and less "important" men, the division of labor among families, the ritual context of every act.

When completed, the dance house became the center of a village's social and religious activities. In both its construction and in its later use it united the various families into a symbolic whole. During the sacred dances that would be held for years to come, the dance house would continue to unite people with one another—and with the spirit world as well.

IV: Old Age and Death

At the time of death,
When I found there was to be death,
I was very much surprised.
All was failing.
My home,
I was sad to leave it.

I have been looking far,
Sending my spirit north, south, east,
    and west,
Trying to escape from death,
But could find nothing,
No way of escape.

Song of the Spirit,
Luiseño

The Men I Knew

Throughout California the chief, almost always a moralist, would lecture and harangue the people: be industrious, he would tell them; be moderate, be peaceful, be loyal to family. Everyone shared these values, but of course not everyone lived up to them. (If everyone were perfectly virtuous why would the chief have to harangue?) Personalities within a tribal group varied widely. Some people were kindly, others prone to violence; some foolish and others wise. Thus when a Hupa man talked candidly about his acquaintances, he described not a "typical" Hupa—such a person exists only in the imagination—but rather an amazing range of unique individuals.

Captain John was a good man. He was sort of a religious fellow like a preacher, and he always talked to the people. Old John told them how to act, what to say, and things like that. He was good to everyone. The other people depended on John some. He always was good to them. He knew the laws, and he told others about them. He was always telling young folks what was right and what was wrong. Anything he had, he divided up with others. Sometimes he would get a whole boatload of eels or salmon and give them all away. He gave them to the old people, every one. Old John would give away the last thing he had. He was a good man, but if you got into trouble with him, look out! He didn't stand back for no one....

Captain John's brother was a good man, but sometimes he would get crazy mad. He would get sore at some little thing, and that would start him off. He would beat up his wives and if anyone said anything to him, he would beat them up too. Once he got mad and threw everything in his house in the river. Other times he was a nice fellow, but once in a while he would get on them spells....

S——'s father was the richest man in Hupa. That old man had enough stuff for two dances, a lot of white deerskins and other stuff. He was a good old fellow. Good and generous too. You can't say that for S——. I don't know where he got his ways, but he is sort of selfish, a stingy person. He got all that stuff of his father's that was left. He still got a lot of it, but he's a man who never gives a dance. He's too stingy. If he gave a dance he would have to feed all those people. He lends the stuff to other people who give dances. That's the way he's done all these years. He's good to no one. His father was a different man....

There were some tough fellows in those days. Always getting into trouble. There was a man down on the Klamath named Tipsa Frank [a Yurok] who was bad. If he had anything against a man he would kill him. Everyone was afraid to tackle him. They thought for a while that he had a good dream and couldn't be killed. Finally he did so much someone killed him. I never knew anyone that tough here in Hupa, but there were pretty bad ones sometimes. Rule is they didn't last long. Someone always killed them. When they settled for a man like that, a little pay was good enough. He was better off dead....

There was an old fellow when I was a boy who had been in a lot of battles. His name was Rennert. He was no man to fool with. He never said much about what he did, but I heard a lot about him from other folks. Once there was a fight down at the Hostler Ranch. There was a little Indian there. Pretty brave man. Rennert and his bunch came down from the side hill and started fighting. That little Hostler Indian kept coming closer. Rennert came closer too. They kept shooting at each other, but they kept dodging the arrows. Rennert wanted to get close enough to him to take after him with a knife. All the others stood back to see what would happen. Then the Hostler people yelled that their fellow was getting too close. He put his arrows in his arrow case and ran back. Rennert pulled out his knife and ran after him. That little fellow ran so fast that Rennert couldn't catch him. A fellow like Rennert has to have confidence in himself to be brave like that....

Some fellows were cowards. They didn't like to fight or get into trouble at all. Fellows like that tried to keep out of the way so they would have no trouble. P——'s father was a coward. I saw men call him down several times. He wouldn't ever fight. Pretty husky fellow, too. Weighed about 180 pounds. Sometimes it is better for a fellow to back down and avoid trouble, but there are times when he has to stand right up to another fellow....

There was a fellow that lived across the river who talked like a woman. He liked to do women's things like sewing. He didn't do what the other men did. I knew another fellow like that at Captain John's Ranch....

I never knew anyone who was bad-crazy. Indians don't get crazy much. When they get that way a doctor [shaman] tries to cure them. I heard a story once about a couple who got crazy, young couple too. Those people got crazy and kept getting worse and worse. They would eat but they never lived in a house. There is a big oak just this side of Miskut Ranch that has a big branch that reaches out over the river. They used to sleep there at night. During the day they just traveled around. All over the valley. They must have eaten something to keep alive. I guess people gave them food. Must have been pretty strong too to be able to keep walking around all the time. They kept going that way for quite a long time. Finally they must have gotten a little better because some people were able to take them over to Redwood where there was a good doctor. She was a Redwood Indian [Whilkut], but a good doctor. That doctor doctored them and they got straightened out. It took a long time, but they got better....

Sometimes there were fellows without much sense. They were harmless, pitiful. People always treated them good and talked to them sort of nice like. There were lots like that in the old days.

HUPA

Strong family and tribal ties did not make the Hupa into a homo-geneous assemblage. On the contrary, family and group seem to have provided a tolerant structure in which people had the security to develop their own personalities. After all, no matter how odd or difficult one might be, one was still someone's relative, and part of a family that would—unless pushed to extremes—provide care and companionship and give a sense of belonging. There is a complex paradox here: namely, that tribal societies which value family and "fitting in"—societies that specifically discourage independence—nevertheless often provide a network of support that gives individuals the freedom to become unique.

Old Gambler's Song

The experience of old age varied from one culture to another in California, indeed from one person to another. For some it was lonely and sad.

> I am the only one, the only one left.
> An old man, I carry the gambling-board;
> An old man, I sing the gambling song.
> The roots I eat of the valley.
> The pepper-ball is round.
> The water trickles, trickles.
> The water-leaves grow along the river bank.
> I rub the hand, I wiggle the tail
> I am a doctor, I am a doctor.
>
> KONKOW

The "pepper-ball" was probably the laurel nut, and perhaps the fact that the old gambler was eating roots and laurel nuts (rather than meat, fish, acorn bread, and seed cake) suggests his poverty. "I rub the hand, I wiggle the tail," describes motions made in gambling. The final line, "I am a doctor," is affirmation; despite age and poverty, the gambler declares that he still has the magical powers necessary to let him win.

Grandfather's Prayer

For some people, it is true, old age brought pain, disappointment, even bitterness. For others, however, it brought a deep familiarity with the world, self-acceptance, even wisdom. "Long ago, when I was small," recalled a Wintu woman, "I used to listen to my grandfather when he prayed." The grandfather woke early in the morning, washed his face, and prayed. He prayed to Olelbes, He-Who-Is-Above, the Wintu world creator. He also prayed directly and intimately to the things around him—to the rocks, trees, salmon, acorns, sugar-pine, water, and wood. At the end of his life he talked to the world—sharing his sadness and regret—as one might talk to an old and very trusted friend.

Oh Olelbes, look down on me.
I wash my face in water, for you,
Seeking to remain in health.
I am advancing in old age; I am not capable of anything any
    more.
You whose nature it is to be eaten [i.e., deer],
You dwell high in the west, on the mountains, high in the
    east, high in the north, high in the south;
You, salmon, you go about in the water.
Yet I cannot kill you and bring you home.
Neither can I go east down the slope to fetch you, salmon.
When a man is so advanced in age, he is not in full vigor.
If you are rock, look at me; I am advancing in old age.
If you are tree, look at me; I am advancing in old age.
If you are water, look at me; I am advancing in old age.
Acorns, I can never climb up to you again.
You, water, I can never dip you up and fetch you home again.
My legs are advancing in weakness.
Sugar-pine, you sit there; I can never climb you.
In my northward arm, in my southward arm, I am advancing
    in weakness.
You who are wood, you wood, I cannot carry you home
    on my shoulder.
For I am falling back into my cradle.
This is what my ancestors told me yesterday, they who have
    gone, long ago.
May my children fare likewise!   WINTU

The reference to "northward arm" and "southward arm" was typically
Wintu, and its usage suggests a cultural wisdom so deep and unconscious
that it was embedded in the very structure of language. In English we
refer to the right arm and the left arm, and we might describe a certain
mountain as being to our right or left, in front or in back of us depending
upon which way we are facing at the moment. We use the body—the
self—as the point of reference against which we describe the world. The
Wintu would never do this, and indeed the Wintu language would not
permit it. If a certain mountain was to the north, say, the arm nearest that
mountain would be called the northward arm. If the Wintu turned around,
the arm that had previously been referred to as the northward arm would

65

now be called the southward arm. In other words, the features of the world remained the constant reference, the sense of self was what changed—a self that continually accommodated and adjusted to a world in which the individual was not the center of all creation.

Crying

People in these small societies were intimately known and closely inter-connected. When a person died relatives and close friends began the mourning cry—not an ordinary cry, but the keening or ritualized wail that soon rose up from an entire village.

And the first time when I could hardly remember, I think, a person died and my mother was crying. And I was scared. I don't know how old I was, but I was scared. I sure hate to see my mother cry. I think that was the first woman I heard. Maybe I was about five or six years old that time. That was my mother's relation, too, that old man who died. Gee, make me feel so afraid don't know what to do. I was sitting in her lap. And she hold me and crying, and I start to cry too. I can't stop crying, and they had to shake me up.

So my mother hold me in her lap, and I got scared. Never heard her cry before. And my aunt started to cry too, and all the women crying. Women cry, but hardly men cry. They have the tears, but not so loud.   POMO

Death Song

As soon as a person died, messengers were sent to summon distant friends and relatives to the cremation or burial. Widows or widowers singed their hair and covered their faces with pitch and ashes. Women,

forlorn and grief-stricken, often beat their breasts with stone pestles and
had to be restrained from doing themselves serious harm.

My heart is lost, lost.
My heart sets, sets.
My heart goes to the other world.
My heart goes to the other world.
My heart goes to the ocean foam.
My heart goes to the ocean foam. CUPEÑO

Burial Oration

In a world in which each person was closely connected to others, death
brought deep grief—and also deep fear. The fear was specific: namely
that the ghost, cut off from family and friends, would in its terrible loneli-
ness try to capture the souls of the living. Thus throughout California
funeral songs and orations urged the spirit of the deceased to go on its
way and leave the living behind.
  The "spirit trail" (or "flower trail," as it was sometimes called)
mentioned in the following oration was the Milky Way, which, according
to the Wintu, was the roadway to the land of the dead.

You are dead.
You will go above there to the trail.
That is the spirit trail.
Go there to the beautiful trail.
May it please you not to walk about where I am.
You are dead.
Go there to the beautiful trail above.
That is your way.
Look at the place where you used to wander.
The north trail, the mountains where you used to wander,
    you are leaving.
Listen to me: go there! WINTU

The Land of the Dead

Images of the afterworld varied from group to group. The Maidu felt that virtuous souls traveled to a paradise of pleasure. Most Native Californians, however, viewed the afterworld as a drab, gloomy place (at least by living people's standards) where everything was the reverse of what it was in the land of the living. In the "Orpheus" story that follows, dead people's days are really years, their deer are beetles, and things are visible only during the darkness of night. Death here is seen not as the absence of life, but rather as the mirror image of life.

A great hunter brought home a wife. They loved each other, and were very happy. But the man's mother hated the young wife, and one day when the husband was out hunting, she put a sharp pointed object in the wife's seat, and the woman sat down upon it and was killed.

The people immediately brought brush and piled it up. They put her body upon it, and burned it, so that when her husband returned that night the body was all consumed.

The man went to the burning-place, and stayed there motionless. Curls of dust rose and whirled about the charred spot. He watched them all day. At night they grew larger, and at last one larger than all the rest whirled round and round the burned spot, and set off down the road. The man followed it. At last when it was quite dark, he saw that it was the figure of his wife that he was following, but she would not speak to him.

She was leading him in the direction of the rock past which all dead people must go. If they have been bad in their lives, the rock falls on them and crushes them. When they came to this rock, she spoke to him. "We are going to the place of dead people," she told him. "I will take you on my back so that you will not be seen and recognized as one of the living."

Thus they went on until they came to the river the dead have to ford. This was very dangerous, because the man was not dead, but the woman kept him on her back, and they came through safely. The woman went directly to her people. She went home to her parents and brothers and sisters who had died before. They were glad to see her, but they did not like the man for he was not dead. The woman pleaded for him, however, and they let him stay. Special food had to be always cooked for him, for he could not eat what dead people live on. Also in the daytime he could see nothing; it was as if he were alone all day long; only in the night could he see.

When the people were going hunting, they said to each other that they ought to take the man along. So they took him, and stationed him on the trail the deer would take. Presently he heard them shouting, "The deer, the deer," and he knew they were shouting to him that the deer were coming in his direction. But he could see nothing. Then he looked again, and he could see two little black beetles; he knocked them over, and these were the deer the dead people hunted. And when all the people had come up, they praised him for his hunting, and after that they did not complain of his being there.

The people were sorry for him. They said, "It is not time for him to die yet. He has a hard time here. The woman ought to go back with him." So they planned that it should be so. They instructed the man and the woman to have nothing to do with each other for three nights after their return to earth; but three nights for the dead meant three years for the living.

So the man and the woman returned to earth, and they were continent for three nights. But they did not know that the dead people meant three years, and when the husband woke on the morning of the fourth day he was alone. SERRANO

Summons to a Mourning Ceremony

Throughout much of California people held annual mourning ceremonies to honor those who had died during the previous year. Guests were invited from surrounding villages to partake in feasting, dancing, singing, ritual washing and crying, and effigy burning. This was the final ritualized outpouring of grief. Then gifts were exchanged between hosts and guests in ceremonies that bound the living together once again. At the end of the mourning ceremony—which in some places lasted for as long as seven days—relatives of the dead were released from their mourning restrictions. They could wash the ashes and pitch from their faces, let their hair grow long, eat ordinary foods, and perhaps remarry. Life would go on.

On the day of the mourning ceremony, a Miwok chief rouses his people to prepare for the guests. He speaks in the ceremonial manner—a ritualized form of speaking as different from ordinary speech as dancing was from ordinary walking.

Get up! Get up! Get up! Get up! Get up!
Wake up! Wake up! Wake up!
People get up on the south side,
East side, east side, east side, east side,
North side, north side, north side,
Lower side, lower side, lower side!
You folks come here!
Visitors are coming, visitors are coming.
Strike out together!
Hunt deer, squirrels!
And you women, strike out, gather wild onions, wild
     potatoes!
Gather all you can! Gather all you can!
Pound acorns, pound acorns, pound acorns!
Cook, cook!
Make some bread, make some bread!
So we can eat, so we can eat, so we can eat.
Put it up, and put it up, and put it up!
Make acorn soup so that the people will eat it!
There are many coming.
Come here, come here, come here, come here!
You have to be dry and hungry.
Be for a while.
Got nothing here.
People get up, people around get up!
Wake up!
Wake up so you can cook!
Visitors are here now and all hungry.

Get ready so we can feed them!
Gather up, gather up, and bring it all in, so we can give it
    to them!
Go ahead and eat!
That's all we have.
Don't talk about starvation, because we never have much!
Eat acorns!
There is nothing to it.
Eat and eat!
Eat! Eat! Eat! Eat!
So that we can get ready to cry.
Everybody get up! Everybody get up!
All here, very sad occasion.
All cry! All cry!
Last time for you to be sad.   MIWOK

V: The Aliveness of Things

Plants are thought to be alive, their juice is their blood, and they grow. The same is true of trees. All things die, therefore all things have life. Because all things have life, gifts have to be given to all things.

William Ralganal Benson,
Pomo

The Pleiades and Their Pursuer

People throughout the world have had stories about heavenly bodies. Stars, planets, or constellations were variously kings, hunters, dragons, lovers, gods, bears—every manner of living thing. To most moderns such stories seem quaint and innocent; stars and planets are held to be inanimate bodies, their motions dictated by certain impersonal, predictable laws of physics. But to Native Californians and others the twinkling of stars, the weaving of planets, the passage of comets, the showers of meteorites, and the stately procession of the zodiac suggested that heavenly bodies were very much alive. Like other living things they had will, intelligence, and history. The Pleiades, moving in a sparkling cluster across the sky, had all the vitality of a flock of birds, a school of fish, or perhaps a group of people.

Paruthvi ("Bright") had a harpoon for killing seals and sea-lions, and Kuchachkoshihl (Pleiades) coveted it. But Paruthvi refused to sell it. He kept it hidden in his house, and would not permit anyone to go near it. Then Kuchachkoshihl called his friends together, and they made a plan to steal the harpoon.

In the night they crept up to the house of Paruthvi. Frog slipped inside and crawled up on the beams above the fire, while Mouse gnawed at a board in the wall opposite the place where the harpoon was kept, and Louse tied the hair of the sleepers together. Down on the beach another Mouse gnawed holes in the canoes that were there drawn up. Late in the night a board was gnawed off and holes were gnawed in all the canoes. Then Kuchachkoshihl reached in through the wall, seized the harpoon, and ran.

The women in the house woke and shouted. Someone threw the embers in the fireplace together, but Frog dropped his water on them and put out the fire. Confusion reigned. The people, at last disentangling their hair and tearing themselves apart, ran out and saw a canoe fleeing in the distance. They too launched a canoe, but it filled and sank. They tried another, but it also foundered. So they tried nine. Then they took the last one, and this very one Mouse had overlooked. So Paruthvi and his men gave chase, but they could not overtake the fugitives. And every night they go across the sky, the party of Kuchachkoshihl ahead and that of Paruthvi pursuing, but never overtaking, the thieves.   WIYOT

The story of the Pleiades is not merely an "origin myth"—one that explains how in ancient times living beings got transformed into heavenly bodies. Beyond just providing an understanding of the mythic past, the story describes an ongoing drama. In other words, the Wiyot did not look up at the Pleiades and think, "Once those stars were living beings." For them the stars were *still* living beings; the "origin myth" explained what kind of living beings they were.

The Lunar Eclipse

The moon, according to the Hupa, was also a living being, specifically a man: not an abstract, ethereal, symbolic man—not a *male principle*—but a real, flesh-and-blood, awesomely powerful man. This man had wives and pets, and like men everywhere he hunted deer. The moon's rising and setting, waxing and waning, and especially its eclipses were dramatic, often bloody events in the man's life.

The one who always travels at night has ten wives in the west and ten wives also where he rises. In the distant west he always comes out to the ocean and hunts the deer which live on the water. He calls them by saying, "wu, wu, wu, wu." He always kills ten and then ten more. Taking ten on his back he carries them to the place where he goes up into the sky. It is there his house is. Then his pets crowd around him, his mountain-lions and his rattlesnakes. He divides the deer among the animals but they are not satisfied with one apiece. They jump on him and eat him besides. They leave only his blood. Then Frog, who stands in the body of her husband, clubs them off and they desist. He goes down in the west, nothing but blood. There his wives brush together the blood and he recovers. He always goes back to the place of rising and there they make him well again.

His pets do not do that way with him every time. Sometimes they get enough and then they quit. When they are not satisfied with the food given them, then they eat him.   HUPA

Sun and Moon

Everywhere in California the sun and moon were seen as people. The Maidu pictured them living in a house where they were subject to all the usual domestic inconveniences.

Sun and Moon were sister and brother. They did not rise at first. Many different animals were sent to try and see if they could make the two rise, but failed. None of them could get into the house in which the brother and sister lived. This house was of solid stone, and was far away to the east.

At last Gopher and Angle-Worm went. Angle-Worm made a tiny hole, boring down outside, and coming up inside the house. Gopher followed, carrying a bag of fleas. He opened it, and let half of the fleas out. They bit the brother and sister so, that they moved from the floor where they were to the sleeping-platform. Then Gopher let out the rest of the fleas, and these made life so miserable for Sun and Moon, that they decided to leave the house. The sister was afraid to travel by night, so the brother said he would go then, and became the Moon. The sister travelled by day, and became the Sun.   MAIDU

The use of fleas to roust the sun and moon is typical of the Native Californians' religious sensibility. Theirs was a thoroughly domestic world. People seldom ventured more than twenty miles from their birthplace. Their major life experiences took place in a village and family context, and it was village and family that provided them with the metaphors by which they interpreted the workings of the world. Even the most awesome mysteries—the regulation of the sun and moon, for example—were understood basically as domestic dramas.

The idea, by the way, that at one time the sun refused to rise or that it rose only slightly above the horizon was common throughout California. One wonders: could it harken back to distant arctic migrations?

The Greedy Father

To the California Indian way of thinking, *nothing* was inanimate. Animals, plants, rocks, trees, trails, mountains, springs, manufactured objects and natural objects—indeed all things—were *people*, fully alive and intelligent, with complex and interconnected histories.

Famine descended, and the people were hungry. A man said, "Tomorrow I'll go fishing." The family went to bed without eating. The next day at dawn he left the house. The sun was rising. It was shining on the water. Suddenly the string attached to the fishnet quivered. A big salmon was in the net. He hauled it out and put it down in back of the fishery.

Then he thought, "Let me cook it! It's because I'm hungry." So he cleaned it. He cut off the tail putting it to one side. Then he cooked the salmon. When he ate it, he devoured it all, and only afterwards did he realize it.

Then he went home. He was carrying just the tail. Some distance from home he was shouting, "Here children, this is the tail! There were a lot of beggars on the way who got the rest."

Then the children ran out. They were shouting, "Hurray, we're going to eat, hurray, we're going to eat."

The next day he went fishing again. Again he caught a big salmon, and he ate it on the spot. Again he shouted, "Here, children, this is the tail! There were a lot of beggars."

Now the woman thought, "He's holding out on us." The next day he went fishing again. She told her children, "You stay here. I'm following him. I think he's holding out on us." When she arrived at the fishery, he had just pulled out a big salmon. He cut off the tail and put it down a little ways off. Then he made a fire and cooked it. He was about to eat it.

The woman ran back upriver. She told her children, "It's really true. He's holding out on us. Let's get started, we're going to leave." They climbed uphill. Then they heard him. He was shouting below them, "Here, children, this is the tail! There were a lot of beggars." It was silent. He shouted again. He ran indoors. There only mice were squeaking. Then he jumped out of the house. He was still shouting like that, "Here, children, this is the tail! There were a lot of beggars." He looked uphill. That is where they had climbed.

His wife shouted, "Eat alone there: that's why you held out on us." He was following them. He got closer. He was still shouting. When he caught up with them, his wife told him, "You're going to be doing nothing but this: you'll be eating only mud in the creeks. But we will be sitting around in front of rich people."

And he thought, "Let me grab the littlest one." He reached out, but the child turned into a bear-lily. He thought, "I'm grabbing the other one." It turned into a hazel-bush. He grabbed his wife: she turned into a pine tree. He, in turn, swooped down there. You will see him like that now. He eats mud on the edge of creeks. [He became a water-ouzel, a small, grey bird called "Moss-eater" by the Karok.] But his wife and his children, when there is a deerskin dance, are lined up [as baskets] in front of rich people.   KAROK

When a Karok woman went out to collect pine roots, hazel stems, and bear-lily roots for her baskets, she moved in an animate and indeed passionate world. She gathered her basket materials from *people*—from a woman and her children who had once been dreadfully poor. By plucking roots and stems she was not harming these people but rather honoring them, transforming them into beautiful baskets that would be displayed during ceremonies, "sitting in glory before the rich people." The woman was thus helping the roots and stems fulfill their destiny. Her relationship with the pine tree, hazel bush, and bear-lily was one of partnership, friendship, even equality; after all, she and pine tree were both women, and could thereby understand and help each other very well.

The Stick Husband

To live in a world in which everything was animate and had personhood
was to live in a world of endless potentiality. The most common objects
around one were filled with power, intelligence, and even sexual desire,
making for a thoroughly unpredictable and magical world.

There was a young woman living with her grandmother. The
old woman was blind. The girl fetched wood and water,
made fires, and prepared food. They lived that way. The
girl collected acorns. In the evening she got wood, made the fire,
and prepared dinner. They lived that way without a man. Quite a
while they lived that way. The girl did all the chores.

The young woman made acorn soup. She went out to pick
acorns, pounded acorns, and leached the meal. They lived that way
for quite a while.

One day she was out after wood. In picking up wood, she found a
pretty little stick, round just as though whittled. She put it in with
her firewood. This stick rolled away from the firewood. She did not
pay attention to it until she got more wood. She thought she had
enough wood to fill the basket. She gathered and piled it and again
put the stick with the wood. Again it rolled away. She got the
basket full and put the stick in again. Then she went home, threw it
down by the door. Again the stick rolled out. She put the wood
inside the house, piled it in. The stick of wood she had found kept
rolling around, rolling here and there.

She thought: "What is the matter with that stick anyhow?" It
kept rolling around. Evening came. She went to bed. That stick
rolled into her bed. It lay there. In the morning the stick rolled out
and disappeared. After a while the stick rolled back with a dead
deer, which it had killed, for the stick was a person.

It rolled around over the deer and the deer was cut up as though
by a person. The stick put the meat in the house. The girl was
helping. The stick rolled around to the edge of the fire as it cooked
meat.

The young woman laid the baskets down for the cooked deer

80

meat. Everything was cooked. She set the acorn mush down. The stick rolled up to the food and away as though eating.

The grandmother did not know about the stick, for the young woman did not tell her. She gave her grandmother some meat on a basket plate. The old lady did not know what to make of it, for they had had no meat before. The girl said: "I did not tell you everything." The other day I was getting wood. I found a stick, a nice pretty little stick. I did not know I had found a man. I picked up the stick not knowing it was a man."

Then they ate the meat. The grandmother said: "Grandchild, you did well."

They lived that way. The stick of wood rolled out when going hunting. After killing deer, it would roll home. When wood was needed, the stick would roll out and all the wood would come to the door. They lived that way. Everything he did, he did by rolling. Every time he hunted he rolled out.

Night would come. They went to bed. The stick would roll around, roll on top of her, roll between her legs, having intercourse. The first thing she knew she had a boy baby.

They lived that way for quite a while. The stick killed deer and got wood and acorns. Pretty soon she was pregnant again. She bore a girl. She thus had two children by the stick.   COAST YUKI

Not only was the stick a *person*, but the story itself was a kind of person as well—a rather fussy person who demanded proper treatment. The narrator dared summon the story only at night and only during the winter; otherwise the story might turn on the narrator and cause him or her to become hunchbacked. If the teller omitted any detail, the story would cause illness. When finished with the telling, the narrator would turn attention away from the audience and address the story directly: "Well, it is done," the narrator would say. "You go back into the rock hole." Like everything else in the world the story was magically alive, possessing will, intelligence, and the power to do good or harm. Like everything else in the world, the story had to be treated respectfully—indeed, like a living person.

The Girl Who Married Rattlesnake

The perception that everything in the world was alive gave commonality to all things. Everything was a person, everything was "kin," and thus nothing in the world was really foreign. Even a rattlesnake was a "brother"—so close to us in nature that he could fall in love with a woman and she with him. Such a love story, inconceivable in our culture, is treated matter-of-factly, with dignity and even tenderness.

A t a place called Cobowin there is a large rock with a hole in it and there were many rattlesnakes in this hole. At Kalesima nearby there was a village with four large houses. In one of these large houses which had a center pole there lived a girl. This was in the spring of the year when the clover was just right to eat. This girl went out to gather clover and one of the rattlesnakes watched her. When she had a sufficient amount of this food she took it home and gave it to her mother.

Rattlesnake went to the village and when he had approached very near to the house he transformed himself into a young man with a head-net on his head and fine beads around his neck. He made himself look as handsome as possible. Then he climbed up onto the top of the house and came down the center pole. He went to this girl and told her that he wanted to marry her and he remained there with the family. The following morning he went home again. This he did for four days. On the fifth evening he came back but this time he did not change his form. He simply went into the house and talked just as he had before. The girl's mother said that there was someone over there talking all the time. She made a light and looked over in the place where she heard the sound, and there was Rattlesnake. He shook his head and frightened her terribly. She dropped the light and ran.

On the following morning Rattlesnake took the girl home with him and she remained there. Finally this girl had four children and as they grew up, whenever they saw any of the people from the village, they would say to their mother, "We are going to bite those people." But she would say, "No, you must not do that. Those are your relatives." And the children would do as she told them.

Now these four rattlesnake boys were out playing around one day as they grew a little older. Finally they became curious. They came in and asked their mother, "Why do you not talk the way we do? Why are you so different?"

"I am not a rattlesnake," she replied. "I am a human being. I am different from you and your father."

"Are you not afraid of our father?" asked the boys. "No," she answered.

Then the oldest of the rattlesnake boys said that he had heard the other rattlesnakes talking and that they too thought it strange that she was so different from them and that they were going to investigate and see just why it was that she was so different. They were going to crawl over her body and find out why she was so different from themselves. She was not at all afraid; when the rattlesnakes all came they crawled over her and she was not alarmed in any way.

Then she said to her oldest boy, "It is impossible for you to become a human being and I am not really a human being any longer, so I am going back to my parents and tell them what has happened." She did go home and she said to her parents, "This is the last time that I shall be able to talk to you and the last time that you will be able to talk with me." Her father and mother felt very sad about this, but they said nothing. Then the daughter started to leave, but her mother ran after her and caught her right by the door, brought her back into the house and wept over her because she was so changed. Then the girl shook her body and suddenly she was gone. No one knew how or where she went, but she really went back to Rattlesnake's house where she has lived ever since.

POMO

The Man and the Owls

Animals, plants, and objects were *people,* and like people they were thought of as belonging to families that overshadowed individuality. In the Wintu language, for example, one would say, "There is *deerness* on

83

the meadow," whether one deer or a hundred were present. In the Indian mind all the deer in the world comprised a unit of which an individual deer was just a fragment. Every deer was linked to every other deer and shared a common deer consciousness. Thus rather than stalking individual, unconnected deer, the Indian hunter was forever approaching *deerness:* if he mistreated a deer or even a deer carcass it was not an isolated act between him and a solitary deer, but a crime against the entire *deerness* of the world. In the future the *deerness* would withdraw from him, or even injure him.

A man and his wife were traveling. They camped overnight in a cave. They had a fire burning. Then they heard a horned owl (*hutulu*) hoot. The woman said to her husband: "Call in the same way. He will come and you can shoot him. Then we will eat him for supper." The man got his bow and arrows ready and called. The owl answered, coming nearer. At last it sat on a tree near the fire. The man shot. He killed it. Then his wife told him: "Do it again. Another one will come." Again he called and brought an owl and shot it. He said: "It is enough now." But his wife said: "No. Call again. If you call them in the morning they will not come. We have had no meat for a long time. We shall want something to eat tomorrow as well as now." Then the man called. More owls came. There were more and more of them. He shot, but more came. The air was full of owls. All his arrows were gone. The owls came closer and attacked them. The man took sticks from the fire and fought them off. He covered the woman with a basket and kept on fighting. More and more owls came. At last they killed both the man and the woman.   YOKUTS

According to California Indian thought, people, plants, animals, and objects were basically equals. The relationship between people and animals was not one of exploitation, but of reciprocity. People had to respect animals and perform certain rites for them; animals on their part provided people with food and skins. People and animals lived in balance, and to maintain that balance demanded mutual restraint. Animals acted benevolently toward people despite the animals' extraordinary physical and spiritual powers. People did not slaughter needlessly or humiliate the carcass of a slain animal despite humanity's great hunting prowess. To reach beyond reciprocity and demand more than one's due was to upset the balance and ultimately bring punishment.

Initiation Song

The sense of the aliveness and personhood of everything made for an apparently anarchistic world—one in which trees, bows, or pestles might either favor one or hate one. "These mountains, these rivers hear what you say, and if you are mean they will punish you," a Modoc woman recalled her parents saying. To function well in a world of dispersed power demanded attentiveness, spiritual knowledge, and outright luck.

Occasionally, however, a Native Californian prayer or statement seems to suggest that beyond the apparent anarchy people sometimes perceived a mystically unifying force. When a Yuki shaman led initiates around the tribal boundaries to point out prominent landmarks, he chanted:

> This rock did not come here by itself.
> This tree does not stand here of itself.
> There is one who made all this,
> Who shows us everything.   YUKI

Prayer for Good Fortune

The feeling that everything was alive also gave a sacred quality to the world, at times a mystical sense of one's presence in it. A Yokuts prayer ends this way:

> My words are tied in one
> With the great mountains,
> With the great rocks,
> With the great trees,
> In one with my body
> And my heart.
> Do you all help me
> With supernatural power,
> And you, day,
> And you, night!
> All of you see me
> One with this world!   YOKUTS

85

VI: Getting Power

To the edge of the earth
To the edge of the earth
To the edge of the earth
Snap all the people!
Snap all the people!
To the edge of the earth
To the edge of the earth.

Poisoning shaman's song,
Wintu

My Mountain

Trees, rocks, animals, mountain, springs, and other objects were not only alive, but they also had immense power. People sought that power by forming spiritual friendships and alliances with objects of great strength. An animal might approach a person in a dream and offer to share its power. Or a spring might approach. Or a ghost. Or a rock. Or even a mountain.

When I was still a young man, I saw Birch Mountain in a dream. It said to me: "You will always be well and strong. Nothing can hurt you and you will live to an old age." After this, Birch Mountain came and spoke to me whenever I was in trouble and told me that I would be all right. That is why nothing has happened to me and why I am so old now.

Not long after this, when I was bewitched, my power helped me out. I had been visiting one of the villages at Pitana Patu and had started back home to Tovowahamatu when I met a man who invited me to his house to have something to eat. It happened that a witch doctor lived in this vicinity, but thinking little of this, I ate a big meal of boiled meat and then went toward home. After walking a few miles, I became very ill and had a passage of blood. I went on, but became weaker and weaker, and when I reached the hot springs, a few miles north of Big Pine, I lay down under a bush. For a long time I lay there, and when it was nearly dark I got up and said to my soul, "Since my mountain has spoken and told me that I shall not die, why should I die here?" I went on to Tovowahamatu and made my camp just outside the village. The next day I entered the village.

A "stick doctor," who was my cousin and lived at Pitana Patu, was called. He arrived that night and came to my bed. He said: "How are you? Are you still there?" I was desperately sick by now and had hardly any strength to answer, "I am almost gone." Then

89

the doctor began to work. He twirled his fire drill until the end was hot and put it to my stomach until it burned me. Then he worked over my body with his hands. This felt good. But he did not sing; stick doctors do not do this. After a while he said: "Soon the morning star will rise up, and after that there will be a star brighter than the morning star. You will feel better then." It happened as the doctor said. When the bright star arose, I felt better and soon I was entirely well. This man, this doctor, probably helped me some, but it was my own power, Birch Mountain, which saved me....

Once, I became so sick that I gave myself up for dead. My soul admitted that I would have to die. I died and my soul started southward, toward Tupusi Witu. While I was traveling, I looked down and my soul saw a stick in the ground not quite as tall as a man. I went to the stick and dug my foot into the ground about ankle deep. Then I turned to the stick and said, "This is the *muguavada*" ["soul stick"]. I seized the stick and looked back toward my mountain, which was my power. I knew then that I would be all right and live forever, for whenever a soul going south sees the "soul stick," it knows that it will come back.

My soul then came back to Tovowahamatu, and the next day I set about doctoring myself. I went into the mountains and gathered roots which I boiled and put on my sores. Soon I recovered....

My power from Birch Mountain helped me just as much in hunting as in sickness. My favorite deer-hunting ground was in the Sierra Nevada, west of Tovowahamatu, in the vicinity of my mountain. It often happened that after I had seen deer and tried to sneak up on them they caught wind of me and started toward my mountain. I would say: "My mountain, I want you to help me get some of these deer. They are yours and live upon you." After this I always overtook one and killed him while he was lying under a mountain mahogany tree or some other shelter on the mountain side. This happened many times. After such a killing, I remained overnight on the mountain and treated myself to a feast of deer meat. The next day I returned to the valley. I distributed the meat to my people and sold the upper part which belongs to the hunter.

Once when I started up Big Pine creek toward the foot of my mountain, I asked my power to make it easier for me to hunt deer. I said to it: "Now, great mountain, I wish that you would give me some of your deer to eat. You have so many on you. If you would give me some, I wish you would give them at your foot, not far up." Soon I came upon a group of deer at the very foot of the mountain as I asked, and killed one. As I was packing it back to my village, I saw a herd of mountain sheep. I stopped and hid to watch them, and as I waited one came toward me. I killed it with little trouble and went on to the valley, carrying both animals. I distributed and sold them when I got home. My mountain is always good to me.

The deer and mountain sheep were a heavy load, for I had packed them both at once down to the valley. But when I was a young man nothing was too heavy for me. I enjoyed carrying a large, heavy load. Didn't my power come from the mountain upon whose back are rocks which never hurt it? It is this way with me. Once I proved my strength carrying a stump which no one had been able to move. My soul had told me that no mountain would be too high for me to climb, nor any place too far away for me to go to. That is why I have always been able to get to every place for which I have started.

I had two calls to be a doctor. In early manhood I had my first chance. My mountain spoke to me in a dream and asked me to become a doctor. It told me how I should cure. I would not have to dance, it told me. I should sit by my patient all night, holding my hands on him and singing. When the morning star should rise, I should get up and dance a few rounds, and then hold out my hand, when something like snow would appear in my palm. I should place this in my patient's mouth and blow. But my soul refused this power, for I knew that sometime in my old age it would fail me and I would die. I knew the work was dangerous. I had had another dream and saw blood on a rock, meaning that I should be killed if I were to become a doctor. I refused the power because I wished to live to be a very old man. All I had to do was refuse....

Whenever I dream, especially if it is a bad dream which means trouble, I talk to something in the darkness. I talk to my power. That is why I have lived so long. If I had not called upon my power, accident or disaster would have overtaken me long ago. Even when I have sex dreams, I talk to the night, because if I should pay no attention to them, they would continue and lead to fits....

When I die, my soul will go south to the land of the dead. It will stay there by the ocean and I will have nothing to do but enjoy myself.   OWENS VALLEY PAIUTE

The Long Snake

People throughout California quested after power by seeking alliances with plants, animals, objects, and spirit-world figures. It was felt that a person needed such power to gamble well, stay healthy, fend off enemies, and achieve success in hunting, love-making, or other endeavors. Yet quests for power were filled with danger. The "allies" from whom one sought help were not all-wise, beneficent gods, but rather a kind of *people*. Like people everywhere they were often impetuous and unpredictable, a mixture of good and evil, capable of betrayal as well as friendship.

Long ago a person of Saivari thought: "I'll go swimming." When he got to the river's edge, he looked around, and behold an egg was lying there on the sand. He thought: "What a nice-looking egg." He had heard for a long time what a Long Snake egg looks like, and that it is medicine, is luck. He picked it up. He carried it upslope to the living house. Then he put it on the bench above the *yoram* [back wall], he put it in a trunk. They claim that wealth will come to such an egg. He thought: "I think it is a Long Snake egg." He fixed it up good. He knew what it was, and he thought: "How good." He was winning a lot of money all the time, he was lucky.

Then after a while one morning he looked at the egg. Behold it was hatched out. Behold there was sitting a baby snake in the trunk. Behold a little snake, that was his pet. He used to say: "He is good, he is good, my pet," when he was gambling. That snake was his money whenever they bet on the other side.

Then after a while he bought a woman. The snake was already getting big. It was coiled on the *yoram* bench, coiled up in a trunk. It ate lots of food, salmon too, they fed it deer meat too. That snake

92

was already getting big. Then after a while his wife gave birth to a baby. The snake lived there a long time. The snake was getting bigger all the time, every day it was bigger. It lived in the *yoram*. After a while they got to hate it. It was getting too big. It helped itself to the food, to the dried salmon in the house it helped itself.

Then one morning the little girl was asleep, she was asleep in the baby basket. The woman thought: "I'll go and get water." The baby was asleep. She stood the baby basket up by the fireplace and left the house. The man was in the sweat-house. She hurried along fast, she hurried. All at once it was like there was a noise, she had not got back yet, she was coming back close below the house. Then she glanced down toward the river. Behold the snake was going downslope. Behold only the top hoop of the baby basket was sticking out of its mouth. Then there was a booming noise heard afar as it jumped into the river, downslope of Saivari. The woman ran downslope. She thought: "Maybe the baby fell back out by the river." The snake made a big booming sound as it jumped in. It had swallowed the baby. That was the last of it, the snake went to its home in the river. It was getting big. And it could have eaten up all the people in the house. They had made a pet out of it, out of that Long Snake.

KAROK

A Doctor Acquires Power

Almost everyone in California sought power to a greater or lesser degree. Shamans differed from ordinary people in that they pursued power more vigorously than others, cultivated friendships with particularly dangerous allies, and put their power up for hire by others.

Among the Yurok and other northwestern California people, shamans were almost always women. An apprentice shaman—generally a woman from a family of shamans—underwent a prolonged and at times terror-ridden training in which she would dance, fast, and devote herself to ritual until eventually, in a dream or trance, she attained a vision. An ally would appear in the vision—generally the ghost of a dead person, a monster, or an animal spirit—and give the woman a "pain" (*telogel*). The pain was an object—a physical manifestation of power, something like an amulet. In the weeks following the vision the woman struggled to gain control over the pain, to learn how to swallow it and regurgitate it at will. Once she succeeded, she could summon the pain whenever she needed it and draw out of it the power of her dream ally. As her training proceeded she acquired other pains from still other allies, and likewise gained control over them. Sometimes an ally, instead of giving her a pain, would give her a song which could also be used as an amulet to call forth power.

This is how Fanny Flounder of Espeu became a doctor. She told me the story herself, at various times. For several summers she danced at Wogelotek, on a peak perhaps three miles from Espeu north of the creek. It looks out over the ocean. Then at last while she was sleeping here she dreamed she saw the sky rising and blood dripping off its edge. She heard the drops go "ts, ts" as they struck the ocean. She thought it must be *Wesona olego*, where the sky moves up and down, and the blood was hanging from it like icicles. Then she saw a woman standing in a doctor's maple-bark dress with her hair tied like a doctor. Fanny did not know her nor whether she was alive or dead, but thought she must be a doctor. The woman reached up as the edge of the sky went higher and picked off one of the icicles of blood. "Here, take it," she said, and put it into Fanny's mouth. It was icy cold.

Then Fanny knew nothing more. When she came to her senses she found she was in the wash of the breakers on the beach at Espeu with several men holding her. They took her back to the sweat-house to dance. But she could not: her feet turned under her as if there were no bones in them. Then the men took turns carrying her on their backs and dancing with her. Word was sent to her father and mother, who were spearing salmon on Prairie Creek. But her mother would not come. "She will not be a doctor," she said. Most of Fanny's sisters had become doctors before this. Her mother was a doctor, and her mother's mother also, but her mother had lost faith in her getting the power.

Now, after five days of dancing in the sweat-house, she was resting in the house. Then she felt a craving for crabmeat; so an old kinswoman, also a doctor, went along the beach until she found a washed-up claw. She brought this back, roasted it in the ashes, and offered it to Fanny. At the first morsel Fanny was nauseated. The old woman said, "Let it come out," and held a basket under her mouth. As soon as she saw the vomit she cried, "Eya," because she saw the *telogel* in it. Then everyone in Espeu heard the cry and came running and sang in the sweat-house, and Fanny danced there. She danced with strength as soon as the *telogel* was out of her body. And her mother and father were notified and came as fast as they could. Then her mother said, "Stretch out your hands [as if to reach for the pain] and suck in your saliva like this: hlrr." Fanny did this and at last the pain flew into her again.

This pain was of blood. When she held it in her hands in the spittle in which it was enveloped you could see the blood dripping between her fingers. When I saw it in later years it was a black *telogel* tipped red at the larger end. This, her first, is also her strongest pair of pains. About it other doctors might say, *"Skui ketsemin kel"* (Your pain is good). They say that sort of thing to each other when one doctor has seen a pain in a patient but has been unable to remove it and the next doctor succeeds in sucking it out. The words of Fanny's song when she sucks out blood with her strongest power are: *"Kitelkel wesona-olego kithonoksem"* (Where the sky moves up and down you are traveling in the air).

Now after a time an old kinsman at Espeu was sick in his knee. The other doctors there, who were also his kin, said, "Let the new doctor treat him." Her mother wanted her to undertake it but warned her not to try to sing in curing until she told her to. So she treated the old man without singing; and then she took on other light cases. Altogether she doctored seven times before she sang. Then her mother told her to try to sing, and the song came to her of itself.

Next summer she was at the same place on the hill, again dancing for more power. She was stretching out her hands in different directions when she saw a *tspegyi* [Cooper's hawk] soaring overhead. She became drowsy, lay down, and dreamed. She saw the hawk alight and turn into a person about as tall as a ten-year old boy, with a marten skin slung on his back. He said, "I saw you and came to help you. Take this." And he reached over his shoulder, took something out of his marten skin, and gave her something which she could not see; but she swallowed it. At once she became unconscious.

95

At Espeu they heard her coming downhill singing. As she ran past the sweat-house the people seized her and put her into it and she danced and came to her senses again. This *telogel* took her less long to learn to control. It is her second strongest pain. After she had taken it out and reswallowed it she saw that it looked like a dentalium.

Now when she is called on to doctor, if she sees a hawk overhead while she is on her way she knows she will be able to cure, even if she has not seen the patient. If she does not see the hawk the case is serious and the patient may die.

The song she got from the hawk is also about the ocean or something near it. When she is not in the trance state she can hardly remember the song, but when in a trance she sings it without knowing it.

When Fanny first told me about her power, she told me only about the hawk. She was saving out how she got her first and strongest pain. That is the way doctors do: they do not give it all away. Nevertheless, other doctors soon find out that a doctor has additional pains, from what they see she can do and they cannot.

All her other pains came to her later and are smaller and weaker. She did not have to dance at Wogelotek for these; she dreamed and got them at home. That is the way it is with all doctors.   YUROK

How I Got My Powers

A shaman's training was strenuous, dangerous, and prolonged. As an inducement to persevere, an apprentice shaman from northwestern California keeps visualizing the money (dentalia shells) she will receive when she becomes a full-fledged doctor.

I began with a dream. At that time I was already married at Sregon. In the dream I was on Bald Hills. There I met a Chilula man who fed me deer meat that was black with blood. I did not know the man, but he was a short-nosed person. I had this dream in the autumn, after we gathered acorns.

In the morning I was ill. A doctor was called in to treat me and diagnosed my case. Then I went to the sweat-house to dance for ten nights. This whole time I did not eat. Once I danced until I became unconscious. They carried me into the living house. When I revived I climbed up the framework of poles for drying fish, escaped through the smokehole, ran to another sweat-house, and began to dance there.

On the tenth day, while I was dancing, I obtained control of my first pain. It came out of my mouth looking like a salmon liver, and as I held it in my hands blood dripped from it to the ground. This is what I had seen in my dream on Bald Hills. I then thought that it was merely venison. It was when I ate the venison [in the dream] that the pain entered my body.

On the eleventh day I began to eat again, but only a little.

All that winter I went daily high up on the ridge to gather sweat-house wood and each night I spent in the sweat-house. All this time I drank no water. Sometimes I walked along the river, put pebbles into my mouth and spat them out. Then I said to myself, "When I am a doctor I shall suck and the pains will come into my mouth as cool as these stones. I shall be paid for that." When day broke I would face the door of the sweat-house and say: "A long dentalium is looking in at me." When I went up to gather wood, I kept saying: "The dentalium has gone before me; I see its tracks." When I had filled my basket with wood, I said: "That large dentalium, the one I am carrying, is very heavy." When I swept the platform before the sweat-house clean with a branch, I said: "I see dentalia. I see dentalia. I am sweeping them to both sides of me." So whatever I did I spoke of money constantly.

My sleeping place in the sweat-house was *atserger*. This is the proper place for a doctor. I was not alone in the sweat-house. Men were present to watch, for fear I might lose my mind and do myself some harm.

Thus, once while the others slept, I dreamed I saw an *uma'a* [monster] coming. One of his legs was straight, the other bent at the knee, and he walked on this knee as if it were his foot, and had only one eye. Then I shouted, dashed out, and ran down along the river. My male relatives pursued me and brought me back

97

unconscious. Then I danced for three nights more. At this time I received my four largest pains. One of these is blue, one yellowish, another red, and the fourth white. Because I received these in dreaming about the *uma'a* they are the ones with which I cure sickness caused by an *uma'a*.

My smaller pains are whitish and less powerful. It is they that came to me in my first period of training. The pains come and go from my body. I do not always carry them with me. Today they are inside of me.

Again, not long after, I went to the creek which flows in above Nohtsku'm. I said to myself: "When people are sick, I shall cure them if they pay me enough." Then I heard singing in the gully. That same song I now sing in doctoring, but only if I am paid sufficiently. After this I danced again for ten days.

In my dancing I could see various pains flying above the heads of the people. Then I became beyond control trying to catch them. Some of the pains were very hard to drive away. They kept coming back, hovering over certain men. Such men were likely to be sick soon. Gradually I obtained more control of my pains, until finally I could take them out of myself, lay them in a basket, set this at the opposite end of the sweat-house, and then swallow them from where I stood. All this time I drank no water, gathered firewood for the sweat-house, slept in this, and constantly spoke to myself of dentalium money. Thus I did for nearly two years. Then I began to be ready to cure. I worked hard and long at my training because I wished to be the best doctor of all. During all this time, if I slept in the house at all, I put angelica root at the four corners of the fireplace and also threw it into the blaze. I would say: "This angelica comes from the middle of the sky. There the dentalia and woodpecker scalps eat its leaves. That is why it is so withered." Then I inhaled the smoke of the burning root. Thus the dentalia would come to the house in which I was. My sweating and refraining from water were not for the entire two years, but only for ten days at a time again and again. At such periods I would also gash myself and rub in young fern fronds.

In the seventh moon, after nearly two years, I stopped my

training. Then the *ukwerhkwer teilogitl* formula was made for me and we danced about the fire. This cooked me, cooked my pains in me, and after this I was done and did not train any more.

When I am summoned to a patient I smoke and say to myself: "I wish you to become well because I like what they are paying me." If the patient dies, I must return the payment. Then I begin to doctor. After I have danced a long time I can see all the pains in the sick person's body. Sometimes there are things like bulbs growing in a man, and they sprout and flower. These I can see but cannot extract. Sometimes there are other pains which I cannot remove. Then I refer the sick person to another doctor. But the other doctor may say: "Why does she not suck them out herself? Perhaps she wishes you to die." Sometimes a doctor really wishes to kill people. Then she blows her pains out through her pipe, sending them into the person that she hates.   YUROK

"Pains," to repeat, are physical manifestations of power. Good pains are those which the shaman learns to control and which once mastered enable her to cure disease. Bad pains are manifestations of malignant power, and these are the ones seen hovering about patients' heads.

The shaman, like all Yurok, appears obsessed with money, but money had a different meaning for the Yurok than it has for us. Money was dentalia shells, and dentalium (like everything else in the world) was a living being. A person could thus talk to money, plead with it, cultivate an acquaintance with it. Yet dentalium—no matter how ardently it was wooed—was not very easy to get along with; it was seen as fastidious, even snobbish. It preferred to keep company only with proper and successful people, those who had fulfilled their social obligations and who had high standing in the community. Thus the shaman's constant visualizing of money was more than just greed. It was, in effect, a whole-hearted, single-minded wishing to be a skillful and highly respected doctor—to be someone worthy of dentalium. Such desire was as necessary a part of Yurok shamanism as the mystical visions and ecstatic experiences.

Portrait of a Poisoner

Illness—or at least one class of illness—was generally seen as a physical object (variously called a "pain," "poison," or "bad medicine") which had been magically shot into the body by an enemy or by a shaman who had been hired for the deed. Once the disease lodged in the body another shaman had to be engaged to find it and suck it out.

A man's father, when he begins to make him a poison shaman, places a crystal on the left hand of his son. After placing it there, he makes him eat the root of a plant with poisonous properties. The father takes his son into the brush, he does not eat anything for a day. He gives him porcupine quills, and he sticks a feather into the ground at a distance.

"Hit that!" he says, "Hit that!" giving him the porcupine quills. He shoots the feather with the porcupine quills. Then he scatters earth upon it, and he calls the feather by name, as he scatters earth upon it....

[A man who is a poisoner] must live far away from everyone. He must go out there near the place where he is living, and when he gets there he rolls a log about. He shouts, he hates to let his poison go. The poison is like fire. He calls the name of the one he is poisoning. He commands the poison, "Go to his head!" he says. Sometimes he says: "Go to his breast!" To whatever place is mentioned, there goes the poison.

After poisoning and killing someone, he cries for the man more than anyone, he grieves for the one he kills.   MIWOK

Poisoning shamans were feared and hated, yet they were also accepted as a necessary and inevitable part of life. The poisoning shamans' skills were for hire, and in these small societies that stressed obedience, moderation, and accomodation sorcery was the last resort of people who felt themselves badly treated.

The idea that illness was caused by enemies tended to make people wary of each other—especially of strangers—and it gave many Native Californians a cautious and suspicious cast of mind. Yet fear of being poisoned also encouraged people to be courteous and to keep social commitments, since any person whom one had inadvertently insulted could take vengeance by hiring a poisoning shaman. Sickness, in other words—like one's very identity—was seen largely as a social condition; to maintain good health required that one maintain good relationships with other people—a powerful and pervasive impetus to virtuous behavior.

A Fearful Encounter

While common diseases were the result of "poisons" that had been purposefully shot into the body, there were other illnesses—especially shock—that resulted from hapless encounters with the spirit world. Shamans tended to specialize in one or the other kind of sickness. Among the Cahto, sucking doctors cured "inside" illness that had been caused by the penetration of a "poison." Dancing and singing doctors attended to "outside" (or fright) sickness brought on by confrontation with spirit beings.

We were killing lizards. I was carrying the sack. We had many of them. The sack was full. My companion killed a small one. Its mother ran off and lay near by. "Where is the big one lying?" he asked me.

"There it is," I said.

He was about to shoot it.

"Do not kill me. Already you have killed my little one. I would live," she said.

Fire burst out of its mouth. I dropped the load in the sack and ran up the hill. I was sick. They doctored me. I didn't know anything because I had died. I heard my mother when she cried and said, "My little boy." It was very dark. My father and mother were standing there. I was standing at the base of the rock behind a bush.

From the north something flew there. It spit over me.

"Your feathers will grow. You will fly up in the sky. There are flowers there. It is a good place. There is sunshine. It is a good land."

Again, a large one flew there.

"Have you fixed him already?" he asked.

101

"Yes, I fixed him some time ago. Why have not the feathers come out?"

"Listen, two are doctoring him. Well, we must leave him. Make him fly up now."

I fell back because I did not know how to fly. I did not go anywhere. I was senseless right there. That is all.   CAHTO

Searching After a Soul

Another major kind of illness was caused by ghosts—*halyatsxamn huthao* (soul-taking), as the Yuma called it, when the ghosts of dead relatives tried to steal the soul of a living person. In many parts of California shamans specialized in the diagnosis and cure of the much dreaded ghost diseases.

It sometimes happens that a man drops down dead [unconscious] and may be in that condition for days. The soul has been taken away by that of a relative who wants it with him in the spirit world. I remember it happening when I was a young man. They got a ghost-doctor because the man had not been sick at all.

The doctor came about midday and stretched the body out in the open with the head lying to the east. He built four little hills of sand in a line stretching away from his feet to the west. He stood near the westernmost hill and took out of his bag cane tubes with tobacco in them. Carrying these he walked in a wide circle around the man, singing as he went. He stopped where he had begun and laid the tubes at his feet. Then he picked up one, lit it and smoked. In one whiff all the tobacco had gone. But no smoke came out of his mouth. In a minute the smoke began to come out of the hill nearest to the dead. He repeated this four times, walking around, singing, smoking and making smoke come out of the hills one after another. When he had finished he waited awhile and then said that the dead man's soul could not be found in the spirit world, that no one knew about it. He said that the spirits had not taken it, and perhaps the cause of the illness was witchcraft.   YUMA

102

The Rainmaker

Aside from curing, shamans had a variety of other powers. The rainmaking shaman was especially prominent among the farming groups of the Colorado River. Generally these people depended upon the river's spring floods. The water subsided throughout the summer, laying down a thick, rich blanket of mud in which people planted corn, beans, pumpkins, melons, and native grains. In most years the crops grew prodigiously under the hot desert sun. Sometimes, however, the river failed to rise sufficiently; people looked anxiously to the sky for rain—and, ultimately, they looked to the rainmaker.

T he last rainmaker we had was an old man named Silutha-up who belonged to the Liots Kwestamuts [clan]. It was a very religious clan and its members had very powerful dreams. People said it was different from the other clans because in the old days it treated the dead in a different way. Instead of cremating, a special shelter was built. The dead man was put with his back against one of the center posts in a sitting position and the body was left there to rot.

I remember a time when there was no rain for two years and the flood was very low. There was very little overflow. Everybody got very worried and all the men got together. They decided to send for this old man who was living out to the west at the foot of the mesa. He sent a message telling them to place four bamboo tubes filled with tobacco in the middle of the big shelter where the meeting was held; to build a fire close by them and let it die away into embers.

When he came to the place hundreds of people had gathered around. He picked up the tubes one at a time and smoked them very quickly. He made a short speech, saying that it was the spirit Turtle (*Kupet*) that had given him the power on the mountain Amyxape. The spirit had shown him exactly what to do and had told him to think of the Turtle and name him when he performed the ritual. He commanded the people to follow him out of the shelter and run in a body towards the north, raising as much dust as possible. This they did and the old man went off home. Before he had gone very far there were patches of cloud all over the sky and rain had fallen in several places. In less than an hour a heavy downpour had begun which lasted about four days.   YUMA

The Rattlesnake Shaman

For the Tipai who lived in the extreme southern part of California and in northern Mexico, rattlesnakes were a fearsome, ever-present threat. The mountains and deserts of the Tipai world held no fewer than five distinct species of rattlesnake: the sidewinder, the western diamondback, the speckled, the red diamond, and the Pacific. In a world such as this the rattlesnake shaman was a figure of considerable importance.

A rattlesnake shaman is called *wikwisiyai*. I knew an old man, Tcipalai, who was sitting, with his two sons, at Snau-yuke. He said, "There goes an old man with a basket hat on his head" [a cryptic reference to a snake]. His son said, "You lie; there is nothing there. We are going to look." Tcipalai said, "All right; go and see. Go close to the bush by the draw." They went where he directed them and saw a snake. They were frighten-ed: one ran off, the other ran back. This man was owner of the snakes and could cure their bites. He was a snake. He could talk with them. A snake would come to him to say that he was going off to borrow something. He really meant he was going to bite someone. But Tcipalai would say, "No: you will put me to a lot of work [to cure the patient]."

Once I was hunting with him. His wife prepared a quantity of acorn mush. We hunted all day but found nothing, neither rabbits nor rats. When we returned to within a mile from home, we reach-ed a large rock, with a hollow under it, standing near the trail. He said to me, "I have a great deal of mush at the house, but nothing to eat with it. I am going around this rock to get some game: you remain here." He went to the other side of the rock, rapped on it four times with his hand, stamped around it several times, until snakes began to come out of the hollow in numbers. He killed some with a dry stick. I stood by, very much afraid, until I was invited

104

around the rock to see. I saw a great heap of snakes of all descriptions there. Then, when he had taken what he wanted, he told the others to return under the rock. I saw him wring their heads off, wrap them in tanglefoot grass, and tie the bundle with his breech clout to carry home. There he boiled them all in a big pot filled with water. I refused to eat because it was rattlesnake, but the man said it was not; it was another species. But still I refused. Rattlesnakes are not food, so I think that man must be a snake himself to deal with them.

From infancy this man dreamed of curing rattlesnake bites. The faculty grew in him. He remained continent until he was an adult. Then, when a rattlesnake bit a man, he told the people that all his life he had dreamed of curing such bites, that he was now going to try in secret. He cured him. Then he took a wife and continued his vocation. No one ever doubted him, because he always effected a cure when he announced his intention.

When I was young I saw him cure a man at Snauyuke. The stricken man was carried to a spot distant from a house (such patients are never treated near houses), and Tcipalai was sent for. Others wanted to watch him, but he forbade them saying that they had been with their women. Menstruating women were also warned away, for such would kill a patient. Before he reached the patient, he rubbed himself liberally with dust. He sang and danced, circling about the man lying on the ground. He had a thick bundle of white sage in each hand. The man could not see: his vision was darkened. Each time the shaman fanned his own eyes with the sage, first with one hand, then the other, the patient's vision cleared. As he circled he kicked the prostrate man; first on the feet. Then he blew over his entire body. He sat there gazing at him a short time, then he turned him face down, applied his lips to the small of his back, and sucked out some yellow matter, the snake poison. He instructed the others to turn the man face up. He sucked just below the navel and brought out more yellow matter and blood, spitting it out. He repeated the sucking at the base of the sternum. There was no sign of a wound [incision] where he sucked; perhaps the poison comes out through the pores. He told the man to get up and take a wife: he was cured. Then the shaman went home. The man sat up immediately. He never even swelled from the poison. Eventually he died of old age: he was never ill again.   TIPAI

Rattlesnake Ceremony Song

Rattlesnake shamans were also prominent among the Yokuts of the San Joaquin Valley and surrounding foothills. Such shamans gained the power to cure and prevent snake bites by cultivating dream communications with the rattlesnakes. The shamans also acted together to conduct public ceremonies which were among the most dramatic events in California. In order to protect people against snake bites the shamans collected and handled live rattlesnakes, often teasing the snakes and allowing themselves to be bitten as proof of their powers. Then they led the entire populace in rituals, songs, and dances. Toward the end of the ceremony the snakes were put into a small hole. Community members approached the hole with sticks, threatening to kill the snakes. The shamans, however, came to the aid of their "darlings." They pleaded with the people and even paid them not to harm the snakes. The people relented, and now the entire community filed past the hole, each person touching it with the right foot. This completed the communication between people and rattlesnakes; in gratitude for having been spared, the rattlesnakes would not strike blindly at people for the next year, but would rattle a warning whenever a person approached.

The following chant was sung during the rattlesnake ceremony. It repeats the mythic words which King Snake used against Rattlesnake in ages past to gain immunity from Rattlesnake's bite. By reciting King Snake's words, people too would become immune.

> The King Snake said to the Rattlesnake:
> Do not touch me!
> You can do nothing with me
> Lying with your belly full,
> Rattlesnake of the rock pile,
> Do not touch me!
> There is nothing you can do,
> You Rattlesnake with your belly full,

Lying where the ground-squirrel holes are thick.
Do not touch me!
What can you do to me?
Rattlesnake in the tree clump,
Stretched in the shade,
You can do nothing;
Do not touch me!
Rattlesnake of the plains,
You whose white eye
The sun shines on,
Do not touch me!   YOKUTS

The Shaman and the Clown

On certain occasions, especially at annual mourning ceremonies,
shamans gave public demonstrations of their powers. Among the Maidu,
for example, shamans battled each other in contests of magic. Stronger
shamans caused seizures and bleeding in the weaker members of the
profession, and as the action reached its climax, native witnesses
reported seeing flames and lights dancing about the victorious shamans,
lizards and mice materializing in the air and disappearing.

Among the Sierra Miwok the contest was between a shaman and a
clown. The clown was a major ceremonial figure in Miwok rituals. He was
introduced properly into the most sacred of dances where he shouted,
"Woo!" (whence his name, *Woochi*), and with hilarious and obscene
gestures he parodied the dancers and even the master of ceremonies. His
body was painted white, and he was said to have had the character of
Coyote: tricky, gluttonous, greedy, foolish, lascivious—and unkillable: a
ridiculous figure, yet protected by sacred powers. Who else but such a
clown would have dared subject himself to the terrible powers of the
shaman?

The one on the far side is the poison shaman, the other is the
clown. Dancing as they go, they come to meet each other,
early in the morning, they leap and dodge each other as
they shoot with bow and arrow. As he dodges, the shaman scatters
earth and throws it at the clown. He makes him bleed at the nose

and mouth, makes him die under the hot sky.

He dances for him, he runs about, he, the one doing the poisoning, looking at the sun. When the sun is getting low, he brings him to consciousness, with his cane he draws him back to life—the one that died.

The one doing the poisoning laughs, as he brings the other back, as he coughs up the poison. He laughs at him, laughs at him, as he comes back to life. He has come to life for good.

The two walk about together, they are partners, they dance together.   MIWOK

At the end of the performance the shaman would have paid the clown for his sufferings; they were indeed "partners."

A Great and Wise Shaman

Today we hear tales of shamanistic powers that perplex the modern mind; we hear of shamans who achieved remarkable clairvoyance and augury, who could eat glowing embers, influence the weather, transport themselves instantaneously over long distances, cure the sick, resurrect the dead, kill by pointing a finger or a wand, command owls, beach whales, turn themselves into grizzly bears, summon monsters, and do all kinds of astounding things.

Jakalunus was the greatest, wisest, and most patient of Indian doctors. Once when Warm Springs warriors came to Modoc country and killed a few men this great doctor sent his spirits to combat them. The invaders wondered why their men died without an observable cause.

Once war broke out with the Snake Paiute. They killed women and children but this doctor's spirits killed all of the Paiutes but two or three who were left to go home with the news.

I don't know what would have happened to the whites if he had been living then.

Jakalunus always brushed his hair at noon with a porcupine brush; in that way he knew if anyone was coming. In his house he had strands of small round plaques, several rows of eagle feathers and red-headed woodpecker feathers, and also stuffed jack rabbits. When anything unusual happened one of these would jump around as if it were alive.

He had the largest pipe ever seen. After he filled it with tobacco it would light itself. A Klamath doctor wanted to trade for the pipe. He was told that the pipe wouldn't stay with him but he was confident of his ability and the trade was made. When the Modoc man returned home the pipe was there. Later the Klamath doctor called and inquired about it. The Modoc said, "I gave it to you. What did you do with it?" "It disappeared." "Well, it got to my house before I did. Here it is. You should have listened to me. Even if you held this pipe in your hand it would leave and come to me. My spirits do that."

"Why can't it serve me in the same way?" the Klamath inquired.

"I don't know," the Modoc answered. "My spirits determine that."

A few days later the Klamath shaman died. Jakalunus' spirit had caused it. The Klamath people wanted the Modoc to kill Jakalunus. They offered many furs and blankets.

An old woman was once buried alive by her children because they didn't want to take care of her any more. Jakalunus immediately went out to dig her up; his spirits had told him about it. While he was busy the Klamath came and filled him full of arrows. He didn't die right away. First he killed many Klamath by snapping his right index finger at each of them. They dropped and died almost immediately. MODOC

Accounts of shamanistic magic puzzle and disturb the modern mind. They run counter to our understanding of how the world works, and many modern people tend to dismiss shamanistic powers as mere sleight-of-hand—deception perpetrated upon the populace by crafty shamans. But Native Californians did not feel that way, and indeed shamans themselves apparently believed in their own and their colleagues' powers. A shaman who fell ill would generally call upon another shaman for a cure, and most shamans seemed authentically fearful and respectful of each other. Among Native Californians the power of shamans was taken for granted—a basic and necessary part of a fundamentally magical world.

VII: Dream Time

I dream of you,
I dream of you jumping.
Rabbit,
Jackrabbit,
Quail.

Ohlone song

Dance of the Spirits

Shamans, and ordinary people too, saw their dreams as passageways into the spirit world—a world where not only power awaited them, but truths as well.

When it was time to gather acorns, all the people of Kamak left their houses empty and went up on Palomar Mountain. An old man named Pautovak came up from the neighboring village of Ahoya, and stopped at Kamak. Finding the village deserted, he decided he would stay all night and go on in the morning. He took one of the enormous storage baskets, *mushkwanish*, that was empty, inverted it over himself for shelter, and went to sleep.

Early during the night he heard the people call out the summons to a dance. He lay and listened. There were children among the people, little boys, and they came near the granary basket. The basket had a rip through which the toes of the old man were sticking out. "A spirit," yelled the boys, and ran away.

The old man could recognize the voices of men and women who had died long ago. He could hear the spirits talk and hear them laugh. One was Exwanyawish, the woman that was turned into a rock, and Piyevla, the man that scooped the rock with his fingers. Piyevla sang that night all the songs that had been his when alive.

The old man could hear the women's songs as they danced. He lay awake all night and listened; till at last, just before dawn, he could not wait any longer, but determined to see them for himself; so suddenly throwing off the basket, he said, "Hai, are you there?" and immediately all the spirits turned into a flock of birds and flew away; and the turtle-shell rattle they had used all night for the dancing he found where they had left it, but now it was nothing but a piece of soaproot.   LUISEÑO

House of Silver-Fox

For most modern people, waking thoughts and perceptions are the only valid measures of "reality;" dreaming is considered less trustworthy, less accurate. To say, "I dreamed it," is to imply that something is false or fantastical.

To Native Californians, however, dream events were at least as valid as waking events. If a man dreamed that someone had insulted him, he would assume that indeed such a person *had* insulted him. To dream of a dead person was to be visited by a ghost. Dreaming, in other words, did not take place entirely within one's own mind; rather it was an act of communication, an important way of gaining knowledge—in some ways even more important than ordinary seeing or hearing because in dreams one came into close contact with the spirit world. Through dreams people met spirit helpers who gave them advice, sacred songs, and extraordinary powers. Courageous shamans might travel great distances in their dreams, associate with the most powerful and dangerous spirits, and see the most awesome and terrifying of sights.

When Silver-Fox left this world, he said to his sweat-house, "Nobody shall ever come in here," and he left a strong wind there to guard the place. No one dares go near this place, for a whirlwind blows up out of it and makes a noise like thunder. Only shamans can approach it; but whoever enters is immediately turned to stone inside. Wolf and Silver-Fox left their power of wind there. Even now, wolves will catch people that come near; and whoever gets inside turns to white rock.

Once a great shaman dreamed of a wolf that was in that sweat-house. He went in. As soon as he got inside, the wind stopped. He went around inside and vomited blood. He said it was an immense sweat-house, as much as a mile across inside. When he came out, he fell down nearly dead. Another shaman cured him. He had seen nothing inside but men turned to stone. Next night this shaman's hair turned as white as snow. ACHUMAWI

114

A Shaman's Dreams

A thousand years ago the Mohave River flowed full and strong, nourishing at least two large freshwater lakes in what is now "The Mohave Sink." The water table was much higher then, the vegetation lusher, and many people lived throughout the area. They supported themselves by gathering wild plants and freshwater mussels, catching fish and wild game, and farming small plots of land. Then the climate changed, an exceptionally dry period became firmly established, and by 1400 the area was a desert—virtually uninhabited and uninhabitable. Civilization retreated to the banks of the Colorado River—a magnificent river 1,700 miles long, fed throughout the summer by the melting snows on the continental divide in western Colorado. Here in the jungle-like growth of willow, cottonwood, sycamore, and arrowweed the Mohave, Yuma, Halchidhoma, and other River people cleared farmland and formed an utterly distinctive civilization. Their passions were warfare, travel—and especially dreaming. Mohave dreams in particular were noted for their haunting strangeness and their deep poetic beauty.

Homyavre, the bug who causes the mirage, came to me one night when I was a small child, and said to me: "I will give you my breath; my breath is cold, my breath is warm, my breath is hot. I will give you my breath, that you may be able to cure sickness."

A female bug came to me and said: "I am the one who made the sun, the moon, the stars. I will give you something. My breath is blue, my breath is green, my breath is red. I give you my breath to cure sickness." This was Mastamho, the creator, speaking through the bug, for Mastamho never speaks to men himself.

A Buzzard came; but his color was not the color of a buzzard, for he was brown. He sang this song to me: "I blow my breath at the darkness, and it disappears like a mist before the sun, and day comes. When you sing this song and blow your breath at the darkness of disease, it will disappear."

In a dream I went to the mountains and built a house. There came a tarantula with a great long beard. It pulled some of the hair from its body and laid it on the ground to represent a sick man. Then it sang: "Come and stand beside me, Boy, and I will teach

115

you how to cure sickness. I blow my breath over the sick one, and he is well." MOHAVE

A dream such as this, like many other Mohave dreams, is striking for its simplicity and elegance of structure, its balance and complexity of symbol. Dreams like this are possible only among a people for whom dreaming was more than a random and uncontrolled activity of the mind; for whom it was an important and well-cultivated art.

Visit to Kumastamho

Dreaming—important throughout California—reached its highest development along the Colorado River. Good dreams were necessary for all endeavors. Dream interpreters were highly respected and oversaw the planting of crops, the forming of alliances, the undertaking of journeys, and the waging of wars. A song or myth was not considered known until it had been properly dreamed.

Before I was born I would sometimes steal out of my mother's womb while she was sleeping, but it was dark and I did not go far. Every good doctor begins to understand before he is born. When I was a little boy, I took a trip to Avikwame Mountain [in a dream] and slept at its base. I felt of my body with my two hands, but found it was not there. It took me four days and nights to go there. Later I became able to approach even the top of the mountain. At last I reached the willow-shade in front of the dark-house there. Kumastamho [the Creator] was within. It was so dark that I could hardly see him. He was naked and very large. Only a few great doctors were in there with him, but a crowd of men stood under the shade before the house.

I now have power to go to Kumastamho any time. I lie down and try, and soon I am up there again with the crowd. He teaches me to cure by spitting [i.e., by blowing frothy saliva] and sucking. One night Kumastamho spat up blood. He told me: "Come here, little boy, and suck my chest." I placed my hands on his ribs and sucked his sickness out. Then he said: "You are a consumption dreamer.

116

When anybody has consumption lay your hands on him and suck the pain out continually, and in four months he will be well."

It takes four days to tell [the origin myth] about Kwikumat and Kumastamho. I was present from the very beginning, and saw and heard all. I dreamed a little of it at a time. I would then tell it to my friends. The old men would say: "That is right! I was there and heard it myself." Or they would say: "You have dreamed badly. That is not right." And they would tell me right. So at last I learned the whole of it right.   YUMA

In dreams the distinction between past and present was erased. In dreams one could talk directly to the Maker of the universe; one could stand witness to the very creation of the world.

To modern people dreaming is clearly set off from waking, but not for the Yuma. As a person grew older he or she often could no longer distinguish between what had been learned in a dream and what had been learned from other people or from direct, sensory experience. To the Yuma the unconscious dream world—timeless and fluid—merged seamlessly with the conscious waking world.

*

VIII: Mythic Time

*Cottontail lived at Black Rock. He
decided that the sun was too hot.
With his bow and arrow he lay in wait
for it one morning in his little cave
in the rocks. He lay there, and just as
the sun came up, he shot it and brought
it down. Then he took a piece of liver,
which he cut thin, and put it over the
sun. Since then the sun has not been
so bright.*

A myth of the Owens Valley Paiute

Birth of the World-Makers

At the furthest reaches of mythic time, perhaps even beyond the deepest of dreams, lay the void, the infinite darkness, the spanless sweep of time before the world was formed.

I n the beginning, there was no earth or sky or anything or anybody; only a dense darkness in space. This darkness seemed alive. Something like lightnings seemed to pass through it and meet each other once in a while. Two substances which looked like the white of an egg came from these lightnings. They lay side by side in the stomach of darkness, which resembled a spider web. These substances disappeared. They were then produced again, and again they disappeared. This was called the miscarriage of the darkness. The third time they appeared, they remained, hanging there in this web in the darkness. The substances began to grow and soon were two very large eggs. When they began to hatch, they broke at the top first. Two heads came out, then shoulders, hips, knees, ankles, toes, then the shell was all gone. Two boys emerged: Mukat and Tamaioit. They were grown men from the first, and could talk right away. As they lay there, both at the same time heard a noise like a bee buzzing. It was the song of their mother, Darkness. CAHUILLA

So begins the Cahuilla creation epic. The creation epic was one of several Cahuilla song cycles recited by an official ceremonial singer, the *hawaynik*. Some of the song cycles lasted as long as twelve hours, and the *hawaynik* had to perform flawlessly. He trained hard, studied long, and underwent dietary and other religious proscriptions before a performance. Each *hawaynik* had under him a company of dancers and assistant singers, as well as several apprentices who were learning the song cycles. The Cahuilla treated the *hawaynik* with lifelong honor, even veneration; for within his songs the sacred knowledge of the people was preserved.

121

The Creation

The Maidu creation epic begins with a vision of the world covered with water. A raft with two beings floats out from the north. A feathered rope drops from the sky, and Earth-Initiate climbs down into the raft. Who made the water, the raft, the trinity of Earth-Creators? Like many California creation epics, the Maidu account seems to begin in the middle of the story. Mysteriously, elements of the world seem to have always been present, their existence apparently beyond question or speculation.

I n the beginning there was no sun, no moon, no stars. All was dark, and everywhere there was only water. A raft came floating on the water. It came from the north, and in it were two persons—Turtle and Pehe-ipe. The stream flowed very rapidly. Then from the sky a rope of feathers, called *Pokelma,* was let down, and down it came Earth-Initiate. When he reached the end of the rope, he tied it to the bow of the raft, and stepped in. His face was covered and was never seen, but his body shone like the sun. He sat down, and for a long time said nothing.

At last Turtle said, "Where do you come from?" and Earth-Initiate answered, "I come from above." Then Turtle said, "Brother, can you not make for me some good dry land, so that I may sometimes come up out of the water?" Then he asked another time, "Are there going to be any people in the world?" Earth-Initiate thought awhile, and then said, "Yes." Turtle asked, "How long before you are going to make people?" Earth-Initiate replied, "I don't know. You want to have some dry land: well, how am I going to get any earth to make it of?" Turtle answered, "If you will tie a rock about my left arm, I'll dive for some." Earth-Initiate did as Turtle asked, and then, reaching around, took the end of a rope from somewhere, and tied it to Turtle. When Earth-Initiate came to the raft, there was no rope there: he just reached out and found one. Turtle said, "If the rope is not long enough, I'll jerk it once, and you must haul me up; if it is long enough, I'll give two jerks, and then you must pull me up quickly, as I shall have all the earth that I can carry." Just as Turtle went over the side of the boat, Pehe-ipe began to shout loudly.

Turtle was gone a long time. He was gone six years; and when he came up, he was covered with green slime, he had been down so long. When he reached the top of the water, the only earth he had was a very little under his nails: the rest had all washed away. Earth-Initiate took with his right hand a stone knife from under his left armpit, and carefully scraped the earth out from under Turtle's nails. He put the earth in the palm of his hand, and rolled it about till it was round; it was as large as a small pebble. He laid it on the stern of the raft. By and by he went to look at it: it had not grown at all. The third time that he went to look at it, it had grown so that it could not be spanned by the arms. The fourth time he looked, it was as big as the world, the raft was aground, and all around were mountains as far as he could see. The raft came ashore at Tadoiko, and the place can be seen today. MAIDU

"As in a dream," is perhaps the best way to describe the Maidu creation myth. Motives and actions are suffused with dreamlike indetermination and vagueness. Even Earth-Initiate seems oddly befuddled. "I don't know," he answers when asked when people will be created, and his making the world out of mud seems a rather homey and spur-of-the-moment affair. The Maidu earth-makers were far from omniscient and omnipotent. They appear, in fact, rather tentative and at times confused—as figures in a dream tend to be.

As for Pehe-ipe who shares the creation raft, throughout all of creation he remains uninvolved—a witness to this most awesome of events, never a participant. His name literally means "Father-of-the-Secret-Society." During Secret Society dances a Pehe-ipe impersonator appeared and played a major role: curiously, that of the clown!

Marumda and Kuksu Make the World

Today when we read an ancient myth we ask ourselves, "What does it mean?"—for *meaning* is virtually all that most translations convey. But for the original audiences myth-telling was a rich sensual event as well. On winter nights when myths could be told, people crowded around the assembly house fire, the myth-teller cleared his throat, and ordinary language—the language of cooking, hunting, child-rearing, fishing, and basket-making—became transformed by poetry and music into the sacred rhythms of myth. In the Pomo creation myth that follows, one catches a hint of the original music that transported its listeners into the realm of the gods. The night was long, and the myth proceeds at a slow, stately, measured pace.

H e lived in the north, the Old Man, his name was Marumda. He lived in a cloud-house, a house that looked like snow, like ice. And he thought of making the world. "I will ask my older brother who lives in the south," thus he said, the Old Man Marumda. "Wah! What shall I do?" thus he said. "Eh!" thus he said.

Then he pulled out four of his hairs. He held out the hairs. "Lead me to my brother!" thus he said, Marumda the Old Man. Then he held the hairs to the east; after that he held the hairs to the north; after that he held them to the west; after that he held them to the south, and he watched.

Then the hairs started to float around, they floated around, and floated toward the south, and left a streak of fire behind, they left a streak of fire, and following it floated the cloud-house, and Marumda rode in it.

He sat smoking. He quit smoking. And then he went to sleep. He was lying asleep, sleeping..., sleeping..., sleeping..., sleeping... Then he awoke. He got up and put tobacco into his pipe. He smoked, and smoked, and smoked, and then he put the pipe back into the sack.

That was his first camp, they say, and then he lay down to sleep. Four times he lay down to sleep, and then he floated to his elder brother's house. His name was Kuksu. This Kuksu was the elder brother of Marumda.

The Kuksu, his house was like a cloud, like snow, like ice, his house. Around it they floated, four times they floated around it the hairs, and then through a hole they floated into the house, and following them the Marumda entered the house.

"Around the east side!" said the Kuksu. Then around the east side he entered the house, and he sat down, he sat, and he took off the little sack hung around his neck. He took out his pipe and filled it with tobacco, he laid a coal on it, and he blew, he blew, and then

124

he blew it afire. Then he removed the coal and put it back into his little sack. After that he smoked, four times he put the pipe to his mouth. After that he offered it to his older brother the Kuksu.

Then Kuksu received it. "Hyoh!" he said, the Kuksu. "Hyoh! Good will be our knowledge, good will end our speech! Hyoh! May it happen! Our knowledge will not be interfered with! May it happen! Our knowledge will go smoothly. May it happen! Our speech will not hesitate. May it happen! Our speech will stretch out well. The knowledge we have planned, the knowledge we have laid, it will succeed, it will go smoothly, our knowledge! Yoh ooo, hee ooo, hee ooo, hee oo, hee ooo! May it happen!" Thus he said, the Kuksu, and now he quit smoking....

Then Kuksu poked Marumda with the pipe, and Marumda received the pipe, he received it and put it back in his little dried-up sack. Then the Marumda scraped himself in the armpits, he scraped himself and got out some of the armpit wax. He gave the armpit wax to the Kuksu. Then Kuksu received it, he received it, and stuck it between his big toe and the next. And then he also scraped himself in the armpits, he scraped himself, and rolled the armpit wax into a ball. His own armpit wax he then stuck between Marumda's toes.

Then Marumda removed it and blew on it, four times he blew on it. Then Kuksu also removed the armpit wax and blew on it four times, and after that he sat down. Then Marumda went around the Kuksu four times, and then he sat down. And then the Kuksu, he got up, he got up, and four times around the Marumda he went. Then they both stood still.

Now they mixed together their balls of armpit wax. And Kuksu mixed some of his hair with it. And then Marumda also mixed some of his hair with the armpit wax.

After that they stood up; facing south, and then facing east, and then facing north, and then facing west, and then facing the zenith, and then facing the nadir: "These words are to be right and thus everything will be. People are going to be according to this plan. There is going to be food according to this plan. There will be food from the water. There will be food from the land. There will be food from under the ground. There will be food from the air. There will

125

be all kinds of food whereby the people will be healthy. These people will have good intentions. Their villages will be good. They will plan many things. They will be full of knowledge. There will be many of them on this earth, and their intentions will be good.

"We are going to make in the sky the traveling-fire. With it they will ripen their food. We are going to make that with which they will cook their food overnight. The traveling-fires in the sky, their name will be Sun. The one who is Fire, his name will be Daytime-Sun. The one who gives light in the night, her name will be Night-Sun. These words are right. This plan is sound. Everything according to this plan is going to be right!" Thus he spoke, the Kuksu.

And now the Marumda made a speech. Holding the armpit wax, holding it to the south, he made a wish: "These words are right!" Thus he said, the Marumda. And then he held it to the east, and then he held it to the north, and then he held it to the west, and then he held it to the zenith, and then he held it to the nadir: "According to this plan, people are going to be. There are going to be people on this earth. On this earth there will be plenty of food for the people! According to this plan there will be many different kinds of food for the people! Clover in plenty will grow, grain, acorns, nuts!" Thus he spoke, the Marumda.

And then he blew tobacco-smoke in the four directions. Then he turned around to the left four times. Then he put the armpit-wax into his little dried-up sack. After that he informed the Kuksu: "I guess I'll go back, now!" Thus he said, and then he asked the Kuksu: "Sing your song, brother!" And then the Kuksu sang [in an archaic language]: "Hoya, hoha, yuginwe, hoya,...etc....etc."

After that Marumda floated away to the north, singing the while a wishing song [also in an archaic language]: "Hinaa ma hani ma...etc...etc..." Thus he sang, the Marumda.

With this song he traveled north, the Marumda, riding in his house, in his cloud-house. He was singing along, holding the arm-pit-wax in his hand and singing the song. Then he tied a string to the ball of armpit-wax, passed the string through his own ear-hole and made it fast. Then he went to sleep.

He was lying asleep, when suddenly the string jerked his ear. He sat up and looked around but he did not see anything, and he lay down again to sleep. It went on like that for eight days, it went on for eight days, and then it became the earth. The armpit-wax grew large while Marumda was sound asleep, and the string jerked his ear. At last Marumda sat up, he sits up, and he untied the string from his ear-hole. Then he threw the earth out into space. POMO

Marumda and Kuksu are strange beings. Far from abstract or ethereal gods, they seem very real, very concrete—right down to their toes, ear lobes, and armpits. The ambience in which they function, however, is utterly magical, saturated with number-ritual, rites, and mystery. Strange yet concrete figures in a magical ambience—the material that myths are made of is very close indeed to the material dreams are made of.

The use of a vulger, even laughable material—in this case armpit wax—to make the world is typically Californian. The use of such lowly matter emphasizes the immense power of the gods. More than that, however, it suggests that even the grossest of substances has sacred potential. Sacredness, in other words, did not reside just in distant, rare, or "heavenly" materials. The most common, mundane things of the body, the village, the earth—these too, in the Indian mind, were suffused with a history of sacredness and power.

Remaking the World

Fossil bones of mammoths, camels, and other strange beasts abound in California, suggesting a previous world. Seashells and petrified ripple marks give evidence that even the highest ridgetops were once covered with water. Perhaps for these reasons California mythology has many tales of prior worlds (often inhabited by "monsters") and of great floods.

In the following myth a bygone world is dimly seen and mysteriously described. The sense of dreaming is exceptionally strong here. Creation and destruction seem to happen by themselves; indeed the dreamer of the old world and the maker of the new world seem passive witnesses rather than active creators, staring open-eyed, amazed, and even helpless as the grand processes unfold around them.

Many people came into existence somewhere. They dwelt long and no one knows what they did. And then one of them dreamed. So he said, "I dreamed; of a whirlwind I dreamed." And they said, "You have dreamed something bad."

Then they all dwelt there a long, long time. And after that it blew, and the wind increased. They had an earth lodge, so they said, "Let us go into the earth lodge. The world is going bad." So they all went in. And they said, "Let all the people together enter the earth lodge; the world is going bad."

So at noon they all entered the earth lodge. Then it blew. It blew terribly. Every kind of tree fell down westward. And the one who had dreamed, that man who had dreamed, stood outside and did not come into the earth lodge. Standing outside he spoke, "It is raining, O you people, and the trees are falling westward all at once." And he went on speaking, "The water is coming, the earth will be destroyed."

And all the houses outside were blown away; none remained. Then, coming into the earth lodge, he said, "It must be that my dream is coming true. I dreamed of wind and I must have been right about the destruction of the world." He stood alone, leaning against the post of the earth lodge. And all the people went. He remained thus for a while and then the post he was leaning on came loose. Then this person went; the one who had dreamed went last after all the people were gone. So the world was destroyed and water alone was left.

Thus it was for some time, and then Olelbes [He-Who-Is-Above] looked down from the north. He looked for a long time everywhere, west, and east, and south; he looked all around in a circle. And in the north, right in the middle of the water, something was barely visible. Then while he was looking, it moved to the west and to the east. He could scarcely see it. Then it seemed to him as if it swam around a little. It was lying there before him on the bedrock. He-Who-Is-Above knew. It was a lamprey eel which lay there all alone. That lamprey had come first into existence, and lay there alone. In the meanwhile, there on the rocks, lay a little mud. The water lay there long, very long, no one knows how long it lay there, and then finally the water began to recede, to go down south, and as it receded it turned into a multitude of creeks. Then at last there lay a little earth that had come into being, and that earth turned into all kinds of trees.

This is all. It has been transformed. WINTU

Woman's Love Medicine

Throughout California the time between the making of the world and the creation of present-day people was viewed as a separate epoch. A race of creator-beings, often much like ordinary people but possessed of exceptional powers, lived in the world and partook in momentous events: the adjustment of the sun and moon; the molding of the landscape; the rescue of deer, salmon, fire, and other valuables from evil captors; the establishment of all human rituals, clans, and institutions. At the end of this epoch the race of creator-beings either withdrew from the world or became transformed into present-day animals, plants, or geographic entities. *Kixunai* is what the Hupa called these creator-beings.

The young men of the Kixunai used to come to a certain rock that stands in the ocean at the mouth of the Klamath. They used to hold there their sports and shooting matches. But notwithstanding all the attractions, a modest woman lived there who never went out of her house. Once, while she was sitting working on her baskets, a beam of sunlight fell on her without cause. "What is going to happen?" she thought. As she was going on with her weaving, she noticed a person coming toward her. "The Kixunai who live around here never come in this house," she said. "Up there is the place they go in."

The one who came in, came intending to be the woman's husband. He lived there for a time. Then he went away and never returned. She heard no longer the sound of the games and the talk of the Kixunai.

Mink came to her one time and said, "You won't see again the one who used to come here. Across the ocean to the south he has two wives. One lies in each of his arms." When she found this out, she was more lonesome than ever. She went outside. "When Indians come," she thought, "they will do this way." She went outside. She looked for the herb with which she was to make the medicine. She looked all over the world for it, but in vain.

Once she was surprised to see that as the lonesomeness fell upon her, the herb grew. It came into the world with lonesomeness. She looked at the ground and saw the herb growing there. She pulled off part of it and took it into the house with her. She bathed her arms and legs with it, and when it was night lay down with some of it in her hand and a bundle of it behind her. In the middle of the night she took the bundle up and put it in front of her.

Then speaking to it she said, "If ten times his heart goes from me to other women, finally it will come back to me. I hope he may be crazy. How many soever women he likes, even if they lie in his arms, this medicine will come to him. Among how many soever of them he goes, thus my heart will find him."

The noise of the Kixunai was quiet. She did not hear their talk. "This way it will be," she thought. "You will hate the one you used to like. Before all others you will think about me. It will be this way in the Indian world, if they do this." When she got up in the morning, she put the bundle of medicine toward the north. The sun shone upon her. "This way it will be," she thought, "if Indians when they come make medicine. But there will not be many who will make it," she thought. "I have made it good," she thought. "This way it will be."

The medicine went to him, and he came back to her. It was the moon who discarded her.   HUPA

The story of the love potion took place in mythic time; but the energy of that event stretched into the present, filling the herb with meaning and magic. A woman who gathered the medicine and performed the rites would draw upon the power of this ancient and mythic event, would feel in effect the rhythms of the sacred era. There was not, then, an impenetrable boundary that separated a "mythic" past from a "mundane" present. Objects and rites of the everyday world were still filled with the power of mythic time; the world of myth was still manifest, alive, and very much accessible through actions and rituals in the present.

He-Lives-in-the-South

The following story is about ordinary things: a woman, a boat, a pestle, a sea stack, a flock of gulls. The emotions—maternal love, jealousy, and anger—are equally commonplace. But the story takes place in mythic time and in a dreamlike ambience. The characters are the *Kixunai*—the ones who lived before the present age. And these common objects and emotions become linked together in utterly wondrous relationships.

At Orleans Bar there lived a maiden. She always brought wood for her fire in the morning before breakfast. The rest of the day she used to spend making baskets. One morning when she was after wood she heard a baby rolling about in a hollow tree. Without stopping to gather the wood for which she had come, she took the baby and carried it home. There she cared for it as if it were her own. When the umbilical cord fell off she considered where she should put it. She decided to throw it into the river.

Soon the boy was large enough to run about. She made a bow for him and put a mark in the house for him to shoot at. She did not go for wood as she had formerly done. She kept the door shut and never allowed the boy to go out for fear she should lose him. Whenever she was obliged to go out she closed the door with great care. After a time he became a good-sized boy.

At a village below Orleans there lived another maiden, who noticed that her neighbor did not go out as she had been in the habit of doing and suspected there must be some cause for it. One day when the foster mother was gone after wood this girl came and sat down by the house to watch. Soon she saw a straw fall and stick up in the ground like an arrow. Watching carefully she saw another one come out of the smoke-hole. Running up on the roof of the house she looked in. She was surprised to see a boy inside. She opened the door, picked him up, and ran away with him. When she got back to her own house she took a little canoe out of the house, put water in it, and stretched it until it became a full-sized canoe. She also took from the house a small storage basket, which contained her treasures. Placing the boy in the stern of the boat she

131

started down the river. They went on down past Weitchpec until they came to the mouth of the Klamath.

When the foster mother came back she saw that the door was not just as she had left it. She went in and found the boy was gone. She looked for him everywhere but could not even find his tracks. She searched for him in the neighboring mountains in vain. "Somebody has taken him away from me," she thought. Taking her stone pestle with her she climbed the mountain on the south side of the river. From its top she saw with surprise a boat going along on the ocean toward the south. "I am going to kill him," she thought, and threw the pestle at him with all her might. The girl had taken a head-dress from the storage basket and put it on the boy. The pestle just hit the end of this and knocked the feathers off. These feathers flew away as gulls and other sea-birds. The pestle stuck up in the water and stands there yet. They went on to the end of the world at the south where they are still living.   HUPA

Grinding acorns was a woman's daily task—tedious and mundane—and the pestle was her most basic and ordinary implement. Yet it too was alive, possessed of sacred powers and a complex mythic history. Once, the woman might think to herself, in the hands of the *Kixunai,* it had been transformed into a sea stack. Who could tell what might happen to it next? To the Hupa woman even the lowliest of implements was a living part of a sacred and magical world in which anything might happen.

The Tar Woman

Indian people in other parts of North America, notably the Southwest, the Great Plains, and Mexico, often had poetic and highly symbolic mythologies. The origin of the hallucinogenic mescal, for example, might—depending upon the tribe—involve the four cardinal directions, the winds, rainbows, magical numbers, the hierarchy of colors, and an array of allegorical gods and goddesses. When the Salinan described the creation of mescal, however, it was with a much different sensibility.

In former times there was an old woman known as Chahe. Her stomach was a basket full of boiling tar which she carried on her shoulder. She would entice people to approach her and then throw them into the boiling tar where they were digested.

One day she was seated on a hill waiting for someone to pass by. There came Prairie-Falcon accompanied by his uncle Raven. They saw Chahe, and Prairie-Falcon said, "Have you got your flute?" "Yes," said Raven. "What charms have you?" For both of the friends possessed magic flutes which aided them in everything they undertook.

When Chahe saw them she said, ingratiatingly, "Nephews, you have a long journey to go. Better get up on my shoulder and let me carry you." So they flew up on their flutes and sat on her shoulder; She was very tall. Then she sang:

Wayawaye! Hesekola!

It is crying, that which I am going to kill!

Then they stood up on their flutes, but Raven missed his balance and fell into the basket of tar. That is the reason he is so black; before this Raven was as colorful as Prairie-Falcon. But the latter reached down and caught Raven by one feather and hauled him out and revived him. Then they pulled out their fire drills and set fire to the tar. Chahe jumped as the fire touched her and cried out, "Oh, grandfather!" Her skin began to peel off and she ran about furiously. She ran into the earth in her endeavor to extinguish the fire, and then came out again. "I am burning up!" she cried.

All over the earth she ran leaving drops of burning tar, and every place where the tar fell there sprouted the mescal. Her course finally ended in the north where she still is heard running in circles. And so she will continue all her life to the end of the world, dropping seeds of mescal. There is still the old woman in the north.

My story is ended.   SALINAN

The image of Chahe, an old woman with a burden basket, could hardly be more domestic and concrete. But the dreamlike, sometimes violent workings of the mythic imagination make transformations. The woman becomes a monster and the basket—full of boiling tar—is her stomach. The other characters in the myth, Raven and Prairie-Falcon, seem straightforward at first, but upon close consideration they turn out to be as polymorphous as dream figures. They must have had hands and fingers, for example, in order to play the flute and use the fire drill. Yet we are told that they possessed feathers and could fly, which would suggest wings. Did they have hands or did they have wings? Were they birds or were they people? In this age before the present age they were both at the same time. The rational mind balks at this apparent contradiction, but the dream mind understands.

Time also has a dreamlike boundlessness in the *Tar Woman* story. The events described happened a long time ago; they are happening in the present; and they will continue to happen "to the end of the world," in the timelessness of myth, the timelessness of dream.

IX: Coyote Tales

A long time ago, when I was a little girl, I used to go around with my grandmothers and grandfather. I used to go along when they went to the mountains, and I used to watch while they panned gold. Then, when it got dark, we all used to sleep in a little house, built Indian style.

Then, the children would all be bedded down and my late grandfather would tell tales of Coyote. He would say to us, "Listen well." Afterwards, with his elderberry flute, he used to sing Indian songs.

"All of you listen very closely," he would say to us, "I am talking in the ancient manner." Then he would talk and tell us many things of long ago.

From the reminiscences of
Maym Hannah Gallagher,
Maidu

Coyote and Spider

Humans first trickled into California 15,000, 20,000, or perhaps 30,000 or more years ago. They hunted with spears, for the bow and arrow had not yet been invented. Without knowing how to make mortars and pestles they could not grind seeds or acorns, but survived by gathering roots, greens, and berries. We know almost nothing about how they lived or what languages they spoke. Yet it is quite probable that many of their stories featured the "Trickster."

The trickster figure was widespread throughout North America and the Old World, ancient beyond calculation and enormously complex. He is at the same time good and evil, crafty and foolish, godlike and scroungy. He is both the prankster and the dupe. He seems to exist in the free and wild area of the mind beyond duality   beyond the trick of intellect that divides things into good or bad, smart or stupid, winner or loser, allowable or forbidden. The trickster is everything at once. He dies, is dismembered, decays, and then is pulled back together again to continue his journey. He exists in an undifferentiated, boundless, intensely creative world.

The specific embodiment of the trickster varies from people to people across North America. Sometimes he is human, sometimes animal, often both at once. He was variously called Manabozho, The Foolish One, The Great Rabbit, Glooscap, Sweet-Medicine, Wakdjunkaga, Hare, or Raven. In California, the Southwest, and in much of Mexico the trickster generally took his name from the sly dog-like animal who skulked around the outskirts of villages, hunting gophers, scavenging the refuse piles, and occasionally stealing salmon and deer meat from the drying racks.

In a typical Coyote story the "hero" sets off on a foolish mission and gets into trouble, as he falls victim to his own irrepressible curiosity and compulsions.

Coyote had a baby and put him in the sun. The sun was so hot that the baby died. Coyote stalked the sun every morning. He went up and up, hunting for the sun, and he wanted to get down. He saw everything at a distance under him. He did not know how to get down. He spit down and the spit fell and fell and fell and Coyote did not know how to get down that far.

Spider came along. He told Coyote he would let him down with his rope if he would not look up and would not laugh. Spider let him down and down, but Coyote looked up and he laughed because Spider's behind looked so funny, you know how it works when he makes rope. Spider was angry and he drew him up, drew him up, drew him up. Coyote promised not to do it again, so Spider let him down again, but Coyote looked up again and he could not help but laugh because Spider looked so funny. Spider drew him up, drew him up, drew him up. He was angry. Coyote promised not to laugh again, so Spider let him down again. Coyote laughed again because Spider looked so funny. Spider broke the rope and Coyote fell and fell and fell down and hit the ground and broke all to pieces. He broke every bone. He was all mashed up. Two girls came along and said, "That looks like Coyote!" One kicked the bones and Coyote came to life again.   BEAR RIVER

Coyote and the Acorns

Those who know Coyote stories only from books can only dimly imagine the performance. Family and close friends have crowded into a dwelling or assembly house and are gathered around a masterful storyteller. The storyteller begins, voice full of laughter and vitality. Now he takes on the character of Coyote, alternately whining, pleading, posturing, importuning, or demanding. He assumes the roles of other characters, he imitates and mimics, he breaks into song. His voice drops to a confidential whisper, then bursts out into a loud and amazing harangue. He ranges freely and widely, opening the darkest fears and most forbidden subjects to laughter. Coyote wallops his grandmother. Coyote makes love to his own daughter. Coyote's penis falls off. Coyote is squashed, eaten by maggots, and comes back to life. The stories are absurd, deeply ludicrous, so profound that they provoke thought among the elders, at the same time so simple that they draw laughter from the youngest child. Everyone—young and old, man and woman, rich person and poor—is laughing together with open, childlike laughter. Coyote stories had morals and deep meaning; but the dominant experience of listening to Coyote stories was the longed-for feeling of being united with others in laughter, everyone liberated and joyful.

Coyote lived with his grandmother. Once he went away on a visit. They fed him sour acorns. He liked them and asked, "How do you make sour acorns?" So they told him how to prepare them. "You put a little water on them and press them down and about two days later you look at them." But Coyote would not believe that this was how one did it. He said, "I think you do it some other way." They said, "No, that is the way we do it." But Coyote would not believe them; he kept asking them how sour acorns were really made. After a while they got tired of his always asking about a different way and said to him, "We take the acorns down to the river and put them in a canoe." Then he said, "I knew you did it some other way." "After you load them into a canoe, you tip it over and drown the acorns." "I knew," Coyote said, "you did it some other way!" "And after a while you walk along the river and you find lots of acorns again."

Coyote believed them and ran to his grandmother to tell her about the sour acorns that he liked. The old woman said, "Yes, you damp them a little and press them hard. That is how they get sour." But Coyote said, "No, I know a different way to sour them. You take the acorns to the river and put them in a canoe and drown them." My! That old woman was angry. Coyote took all those acorns down to the river. He was going to put them into a canoe. The old woman hid some of the acorns.

Coyote drowned his acorns. After he had drowned them he went along the river, thinking that he would find them, but he never found them. He went to his grandmother afterwards and told her about it. The old woman was angry. Coyote nearly starved. Whenever he went somewhere the old woman pounded acorns and soaked them. She had acorns ready now, but she would not feed him.

Coyote made a fire in the sweat-house. The old woman thought, "He's in the sweat-house, I'm going to cook those acorns." And she cooked the acorns. Coyote smelled them from the sweat-house. He ran out. The old woman heard someone coming as the acorns were boiling. She threw blankets on top of the basket and sat down on it. She was not going to let him eat. Coyote came in. "What are you cooking, grandma?" "Nothing." "I smell acorns." "Yes, you have lots of acorns!" He stood around. "I hear something boiling under your buttocks." "No," said the old woman, "I pooped." "No," he said, "I hear something boiling." "I pooped," she said again. But Coyote seized her and lifted her up. He found the acorns. He ate them, for he was almost starved.   YUROK

Coyote's Journey

The Karok, like many other California groups, viewed Coyote as a benefactor of the human race. It was Coyote, for example, who dispersed acorns and salmon throughout the world for human use. The other side of his character—his foolishness, lechery, and utter scrounginess—was also present and the subject of many tales, most notable among them a long, loosely put-together series of stories about Coyote's abortive journey to gather money beads at Klamath Falls.

People who have studied the Karok language have praised it greatly. "Copious, sonorous, and rich in new combination," noted the nineteenth century ethnographer, Stephen Powers. John P. Harrington felt that, "Karok literature, when its syllables are analyzed and the exquisite force and balance of the elements appreciated, ranks well with the literature of any language." To express the vitality of the Karok oral tradition, the linguist, William Bright, has translated the Coyote saga into verse form. The following is excerpted from a much longer retelling.

> A man lived there,
>   he had many strings of shell-money
>   Coyote saw him there,
>   he saw him measuring shell-money,
>   that person there.
> And then Coyote said,
>   "Where do you find it,
>   that money?"
> And then that person said,
>   "At Klamath Falls."
> And then Coyote
>   he went home.
> And then he thought,
>   "I'll make some string!

"I have to go to Klamath Falls!
"I'll go get that money,
     I like it so much."
And he made a lot of it,
     that string.
So he tied it in a bundle,
     that string.
And then he thought,
     "Now I'll start out!"....

Coyote went on upstream,
     there had been a big brushfire.
And he looked around,
     there were lots of roasted grasshoppers.
"I won't eat them."
Finally he went a little ways.
And he thought,
     "I'll just gather a few of them,
          those roasted grasshoppers."
There he was going to gather them.
And then he thought,
     "I wonder why it is,
          I'm not getting full."
And he thought,
     "I think they're coming out my rear,
          while I'm eating them."
And he thought,
     "I'll plug up my ass!"
So he gathered pitch,
     and he plugged up his ass with it.
And he thought, "There,
     now I'll get full.
I've plugged up my ass."
So he ate them—
     but there had been a BIG brushfire.
And he was sticking his butt all around there.
And he thought,

"I think I'm getting there,
        to Klamath Falls"—
                he heard it,
                    the thundering,
                        he heard it like that,
                            it sort of said HUHUHUHUHU.
And he thought,
        "I'm getting there,
            to Klamath Falls"—
                all he could hear was the HUHUHUHUHU.
It was really his ass,
        there it was burning.
It was really the pitch,
        what he had plugged it with,
                there it was burning.
What could he do?
He slid all around there,
        on the ground, in the sand.
And he was just saying ATUHTUHTUHTUHTUH!"
So finally his ass stopped burning.
And he thought,
        "Now I'll never eat them again,
                those roasted grasshoppers.
That's enough, I won't eat them.".…

And then he looked downriver.
There were young women downriver leaching flour,
        on the shore.
And then he said,
        "I'll turn into some pretty driftwood!"
And then he turned into some pretty driftwood.
And then he floated down from upstream,
        he watched them close by,
                while they were leaching flour.
And he said,
        "I'll float to the shore,
                I'll float to the shore!

142

I'll keep floating in circles just downslope from them."
And then one girl looked downslope to the river.
And she said, "Look, my dear!
    Oh, look how pretty,
        downslope,
            that driftwood!"
"All right!"
So they ran downslope,
    they went to look at it,
        where it was floating in circles.
And one said, "Come on, my dear,
    Where's a little stick?
We'll hook it out with that."
And so they hooked it out.
And oh! they took a liking to it.
Oh, how pretty it was,
    the driftwood,
        they took a liking to it!
And then one threw it to another,
    they played with it,
        that driftwood,
            the pretty little stick.
And then one girl said, "Ugh,"
    she said, "Ugh! Maybe it's Coyote,
        they said he drowned in the river, upstream."
And then they threw it back in the river,
    that driftwood.
And they took it up,
    their acorn mush,
        what they were leaching.
Sure enough, in a while, they both were pregnant.
There Coyote floated downstream,
    then he floated ashore downriver from them.
And then he traveled on,
    Coyote did,
        he turned back into a person,
            he turned back into himself....

Coyote wandered around there,
      there was a sweat-house standing.
And he looked inside,
      he saw nobody at all.
And Coyote crawled in.
And when he got inside,
      when he looked around,
            all the chairs were made of pure grease,
                  their headrests too were of grease,
                        and their stepladder too was of grease.
And Coyote was hungry.
And he thought,
      "I'll just taste them,
            those headrests."
And when he took a taste,
      they were very delicious.
Finally he ate them all up,
      he ate up their stepladder too.
Then suddenly he sort of heard something.
And he thought,
      "I'd better hide."
And he lay down there behind the woodpile.
And when the men came back in the sweathouse in the evening,
      as each man crawled in,
            he fell down. [Because the stepladder was eaten.]
And they said,
      "I'm thinking,
            Coyote's wandering around here.
"That's who did it,
      he ate them all up,
            our headrests."
He just lay there,
      he heard them,
            when they were talking about him.
And then they said,
      "Let's spend the night away from home,
            at Long Pond."

And then he thought,
     Coyote thought,
          "They're talking about my country."
And he jumped out—
     "Nephew, my nephews,
          I'll go along!"...

So Coyote went with them.
And finally he kept his eyes closed for a long ways.
Suddenly they paddled ashore.
And they said,
     "We've arrived."
And then he jumped up,
     Coyote did.
And then he said,
     "My country!"
And he kicked dirt out into the river.
And he kicked it out from Camp Creek,
     he kicked it out from Kattiphirak,
          he kicked it out from Ullathorne Creek,
               Coyote was so happy,
                    when he returned,
                         back to his country.
That's why he kicked it out.

Kupannakanakana!
Young brodiaea plant,
     you must come up quickly,
          hurry to me!
Spring salmon,
     shine upriver quickly,
          hurry to me!
My back has become like a mountain ridge,
     so thin,
          so hungry.   KAROK

145

Among the Karok each storyteller had his or her own version of Coyote's Journey, and even the versions were not fixed. On a given night a storyteller might expand certain incidents and delete others, depending upon the mood of the audience or the flow of the story. Yet while there was considerable freedom in telling the story, the closing invocation was ritualistic, and always the same—a prayer for the end of winter and the quick arrival of spring with its edible brodiaea bulbs and salmon.

Throughout California it was generally forbidden to tell Coyote tales during the summer; to do so would bring illness or bad luck to the story-teller and listener alike. Coyote tales were winter tales, reserved for the time when days had become short, leaves had dropped from the trees, rainy days brought gloom and chill, food was limited, and wet trails made travel difficult. At this time people gathered together in cramped quarters to await the arrival of spring; social tensions built up inside houses and assembly lodges. In this atmosphere of constriction nightly fires were lit and people gathered around the storyteller to enter once again the immortal, wild, boundless world of Coyote—fool and benefactor, idiot and god, the one who is killed again and again but keeps rising back to life.

Coyote and His Grandmother

Foremost among Coyote's traits is his insatiable sexuality. He is forever traveling about the world, humping whatever he can find—ludicrously and everlastingly horny. Of questionable taste, he seldom makes love "the right way." Sometimes he fails to figure out the facts of life and is forced into far-fetched experimentation. Sometimes he meets monster-women whose toothed vaginas impel him to take special defensive measures. Sometimes he forces himself upon his daughter or grand-mother or indulges his taste for a variety of bizarre (and in some cases impossible) perversities.

Coyote often seems to be a victim of his own urges. In many stories his penis appears as a separate, independent character with a mind and voice of its own. It drives Coyote to distraction with its endless insistence, its mindless lust for difficult adventures. It habitually gets Coyote into trouble and then—how the original audience must have laughed at this typically male predicament!—often betrays or deserts him.

Grandmother told Coyote to go out and hunt fawn. He went away and he saw new Indian potatoes. He stopped and asked his testicles if he should tell his grandmother there were plenty of potatoes and take her back there with the digging stick so he could catch her and rape her. His testicles told him that he could do that, so he went back and told her there were many new potatoes. She took her digging stick and went with him and began digging.

Coyote said, "Dig down deeper." So she dug deeper and deeper until her behind stuck up out of the ground. Coyote then grabbed her and stuck her head down in the sand so she could not see and he copulated with her. Then he ran so she could not see who did it, but she knew it was Coyote.

She called out, "I know you now, you are Coyote." He said, "No, grandmother, I did not do that to you. I'm going to ask my testicles and penis if I did that to you and they will tell you." So he sat down and asked his testicles and they did not answer, so he asked his penis and it said, "Yes, that is what you asked me."

Grandmother said, "I knew that, I know it now. It is a good thing that I'm an old woman or I would be having lots of little coyotes." She quit digging and went home. Coyote was so angry at his penis for telling on him that he was going to mash it on a rock. He sat down and started to hit it with a rock, but the penis drew back. Coyote pulled it out again and tried to hit it again, but it pulled back every time and Coyote never succeeded in mashing it.

BEAR RIVER

Two Coyote Adventures

Many Coyote stories are dirty jokes—good dirty jokes at that—but they are also much more. A sense of awe pervades even the raunchiest tale. Among some people, such as the Ohlone of the San Francisco and Monterey Bay areas, it was Coyote's mating that was responsible for the very creation of the human race. Coyote's horniness, perverse and ridiculous as it might be, is also full of powerful joy and creativity—as in these two Maidu tales.

Coyote kept going until he saw a place where many women were living. Turning on his tracks a short distance, he said, "Let any kind of worn-out pack-basket come, a platter-basket also, and a worn-out cradle frame also!" Then he saw there all that he had wished for. Then he picked a large root, and pounded it, mashed it fine, prepared it carefully, and when it was very finely ground he made it into a representation of a vagina. Then attaching it to himself, he fixed it carefully, and finished making it. He made a woman's apron, worn out, full of tears, so that when it was put on, it should not wholly cover him up.

And thus he went on. Picking up his penis, he washed and fixed it up as a baby, and placed it in the cradle frame. Then, making a cane from a piece of wood, he went on, walking bent far over like a very old woman.

Meanwhile the women remained there, and just about dark he arrived. Then they said, "Well, this is indeed an old woman to be going about thus!" and they played with the child.

"It does not look like a child," said they.

"I am very weak," said Coyote. "When I picked it up it slipped out of my hands and fell, striking its head. That is why it looks all swollen. Its father is dead. It makes me feel very sad to speak of its father," said she.

Then the child said, "Lbl-lbl-lbl!"

"It always says that and makes me feel sad," said Coyote.

He spoke just like a woman. "Because it cries a great deal, it makes me sad, for I was weak and let it fall," said he. Then they saw his genitals through the holes, although they were covered. All the women saw them. Two of the youngest women said, "It does not look just like a child;" but the others said, "No, it is indeed a child. This swelling is due to its fall."

"That is the head of a penis," said the two women, "that swelled when it fell."

But the other women all believed, and only the two were careful. "Look at her! She is an old woman; can't you see her genitals are of that kind?" the others said. Then these two said, "Very well!" So they gave her some supper. When it grew dark they said, "You'd better sleep right here. You might be cold." So she went to sleep lying in the middle between two of them.

Meanwhile all the rest slept close by in one place. But the two who had doubted went off to sleep elsewhere; they were careful. Then in the night Coyote untied his sleeping-powder, and scattering it about made all sleep soundly. Then, throwing away his disguise, he threw himself upon the women. He kept working until it was nearly dawn, and then went off. Then those women all bore children in the morning; and the children were crying and made a great noise. Meanwhile he went off....

As Coyote went about everywhere he met Cottontail-Rabbit and came to the place where he made his camp. Cottontail told him, "There are many women who dance, but I never go to see them."

"Well," said Coyote, "Are we going together to the dance?"

"Yes! We will dance when it grows dark," said Cottontail.

Then it was night and they heard singing and dancing all about. So they went off, kept going until Coyote said, "Stop a minute! I'll tell you something. You had better stay behind here."

"All right!" said Cottontail.

"You had better stay here. Women are very careful and suspicious of me," he said. "If I have this penis on, they are afraid of me. Keep it for a while. When the women think I am all right, I will whistle. When you hear the whistle, bring it along." So Cottontail stayed there.

Meanwhile Coyote went off and arrived at the dance. He heard the women dancing and shouting. He got there. Very pretty women were dancing. He took a partner there, and two very pretty women fell in love with him. They followed him off. They followed him as he walked about; and when they got near the place where Cottontail was staying, they sat down.

Then Coyote whistled, but there was no reply. He whistled again.

"What are you doing?" said the girls.

"Oh, that is nothing! I am only playing," he said. "I feel very happy to be going about with two women, I feel very good," he said. Then they laughed, putting their legs over him, playing with him. "Why don't you wait? Keep quiet, you two!" he said.

Then, running off up the hill, he came to that place where Cottontail was supposed to be. He whistled. He did not hear anything. He got very angry. He hunted about but did not see him. Then he returned to the place where the girls were.

"What are you doing, going about calling for someone?" they said.

"No, I was not doing anything," said he. Then they lay down beside each other, he in the middle between the two; and they played with him and straddled over him. Again he went off to hunt for Cottontail. Again he couldn't see him, and was angry.

Now, after Coyote had walked down to the dance and left Cottontail behind, two Star-Women came along and Cottontail followed them. After a while Cottontail made love to them, to the oldest woman, making her groan, almost making her cry. Then the younger said, "How can such a man almost make you cry? Such a little man, I guess, cannot make me do that. Such a tiny little fellow can't make me cry!" said the youngest. He then took her, that very one, and he almost made her cry. He made both of them groan loudly.

Meanwhile Coyote-Man kept sleeping with the two women until it was light. Then in the morning he went on; and when he had reached that house, Cottontail was staying there. Rushing in, Coyote looked angry. "I have a good mind to kill you," he said. "Why didn't you stay where I told you?" he said. He was very angry.

"Two women came along and I followed them," said Cottontail.

"Then what did you do?" said Coyote.

"I entered them, with your penis," he said.

"Oh!" said Coyote.

"I almost made the two girls cry," said Cottontail.

"Oh!" said Coyote, "it will make little women cry." He felt as if he had been making a lot of love. Very quickly he got over his anger.

When Cottontail handed it over, Coyote washed and cleaned it with water and put it away. "That is very good," said he. "It is just right for big women." Next day they did not dance, the dance was over. So staying until it was night, he went off in the morning.

MAIDU

150

Coyote and Bullfish

Coyote, at his most absurd, is driven by obsessions, by single-minded compulsions, by relentlessly insistent urges. More than a passive victim of misfortune, he is a talented, never-tiring creator of his own downfall.

Coyote was going up the river to visit someone. He was very well dressed. He had his quiver, bow and arrows, moccasins, and beads. He looked very fine. It was a hot summer day. He came to a nice stretch of sand. He saw Bullfish sunning himself. He was black as charcoal. Coyote said, "What are you doing there?"

Bullfish didn't say a word. Coyote talked and talked but Bullfish never answered. At last Coyote said, "You are pretty small. You are too little to do anything. I'll bet you can't swallow my toe," and at the same time he thrust his toe in front of Bullfish's mouth. Bullfish just turned his head away.

Then Coyote said, "I'll give you my bow and arrows if you bite me." He teased Bullfish that way for a long time. Finally Bullfish nipped Coyote's toe. Coyote did not pay any attention to him; he only continued to taunt him. Soon Bullfish had swallowed Coyote's leg; Coyote became frightened and begged for mercy, but Bullfish ignored him and kept on swallowing him. Coyote offered him all his fine things, but Bullfish just swallowed him entirely and swam off under a rock in the riffle.

The people missed Coyote. They hunted for him and found his valuables on the sand and saw the track where he had been dragged in. So they asked a doctor to find out where he was. The doctor went into a trance and about in the middle of the night said that he was under the water, that Bullfish had swallowed him, but that he was not yet dead.

Then Bullfish made the water muddy so the people could not find him. Otter, Raccoon, everyone hunted for Coyote but they could not find him. At last Mud-Spear [a water bird] climbed a tree and looked. He said, "I see a tail under a rock in the riffle. I am going to try to spear him." So he took a spear pole, aimed carefully,

151

and speared Bullfish right above the tail. The people pulled him out and cut open his abdomen. Coyote jumped out and said, "Nephew, I have been sleeping." WINTU

Coyote and Trap

Ordinary people struggle to avoid trouble, but Coyote works hard and imaginatively to bring trouble upon himself—and often upon the world. It was thought throughout much of California, for example, that the world was created without death, until Coyote insisted that death would be a good idea: it would generate colorful and dramatic mourning ceremonies. Coyote was also often responsible for hunger, difficult childbirth, and other evils of the world. In the following tale Coyote's insistence is strictly comical and self-defeating, but it had deeper overtones for the original audience. For within Coyote's mindless and perverse intransigence lay the explanation for much of the cruelty of what might otherwise have been a more beautiful and beneficent world.

Coyote had a brother-in-law who was Trap. One day Coyote was near Trap. He began to feel around with his foot to find him. He felt all around, and said, "I wonder where that fellow is?" He felt around some more. All at once he stepped right into Trap. Trap caught him and he could not get loose.

Coyote began to plead. He said, "Let me go, Trap. I will not come around any more to bother you." Trap would not let him go. Coyote begged, "Brother-in-law, won't you let me go? I'll stay away from you after this." "No," said Trap, "I am not supposed to do that. I'll get into trouble." Coyote went on begging, and finally Trap said, "Well, I'll let you go just this once. But you must not come back again. If you do come back, I shall not be able to let you go." Coyote said, "No, I promise I won't come around any more. I will go far off and stay there."

Trap let Coyote go. After he had gone off a little way, he began to call Trap all kinds of names. He called him all the mean things he could think of. Trap said, "Brother-in-law, I want you to come around and see me again sometime." Coyote said, "No, I won't come back again. I am going far off now and I won't be back to see

152

you any more." He called Trap more bad names and went away.

As Coyote went along, he worried. Trap had told him to come back and see him, and Coyote could not get that out of his mind. He said, "That Trap asked me to come back and see him. I must find some way to forget about him, and then I shall be all right. I will go to sleep and forget all about it. When I wake up in the morning I shall be all right."

Coyote lay down to sleep. He had a long sleep. But in the morning when he woke up, the first thing he thought was, "My brother-in-law asked me to come back sometime. He said I must come back to see him. I must not do that. I must find some way to forget about it." Coyote went along trying to forget about Trap, but this thing was on his mind. He said, "I will kill myself and then I shall forget about it. I will go and drown myself."

Coyote ran to a big lake and jumped into it. He swam far out and drowned himself. But after a long time, he came back to life and swam to shore. The thing was still on his mind. "My brother-in-law, Trap, said I must come back to see him sometime," thought Coyote. "I'll have to forget about that. I shall have to kill myself." Coyote went along trying to think of some way to forget about Trap. "I'll run myself to death," he said.

He started out to run with all his might. He ran as fast as he could over hills and mountains until he was all out of breath and fell down exhausted. When Coyote came to life again, he thought, "My brother-in-law wants me to come back to see him. I guess I'll have to go back and pay him a visit."

Coyote went back to where Trap was. When he got near the place, he said, "Where are you, Trap? You said I must come back to see you sometime. I did not intend to be mean to you. I have come back to see you. Where are you, brother-in-law?" He could not see Trap, and he felt around for him with his foot. Pretty soon he stepped right into Trap. Trap caught him and held him fast.

OWENS VALLEY PAIUTE

Among the Paiute there was no correct way of telling a Coyote tale. Every storyteller had a unique and personal rendition. If challenged with the fact that others had different versions, the storyteller would reply simply: "Some people tell it differently." Paiute Coyote tales, it seems, were as mercurial yet persistent as was the character of Coyote himself.

Coyote Steals Fire

Along with his sheer ridiculousness, Coyote was also—at least for many groups—the benefactor of the human race, using his trickery for the good of people.

At first there was no fire. Turtle had all the fire in the entire world. He sat on top of it and covered it all up. Turtle lived far up in the east in the mountains. Coyote went there to search for fire. When he neared Turtle's house, he lay down like a piece of wood. The people who lived with Turtle came by and saw him. They picked Coyote up, took him home, and put him in the fire. Coyote pried his way underneath Turtle. Turtle said, "Stop pushing me," but Coyote squirmed onward. He caught on fire. Then he ran downhill westward into this country, where it was icy cold. He caught a quail and with its fat he made the fire blaze up. Now for the first time the people began to get warm. The Mono lived far back in the hills; the Chukchansi Yokuts were in the middle; the Pohonichi Miwoks were the ones who received the fire. That is why the Mono cannot speak well; it is too cold where they live. MIWOK

Coyote and Falcon Create People

For many groups Coyote was the creator or co-creator of the world.

Falcon proposed that Coyote create human beings. Coyote replied that it would mean a great deal of work, but Falcon insisted that it be done. Coyote finally told Falcon how they must proceed.

Accordingly Coyote went out and threw himself upon the ground, simulating a dead body. Presently a large flock of crows and buzzards gathered about and commenced to peck at Coyote's rump. He kept perfectly still until the birds had eaten a large hole in one side and were within. He then caused the hole to close very suddenly and caught a considerable number of them. He took them home and Falcon plucked them. "Now," said Coyote, "we will go out in the country and put these feathers in every direction." On each hill they placed one buzzard and one crow feather. The crow feathers became the common people and the buzzard feathers, the chiefs. As Coyote deposited the feathers he named each place, and on the following day there were people living in all these localities.

Coyote then said to Falcon, "Now that there is a new people, we shall have to become animals. I shall be coyote; no one will miss me. You shall be falcon, and everyone shall know you as chief." Straightway all of the then-existing animal people were transmuted and became birds and mammals as Coyote directed.

MIWOK

In many non-Indian religions, the Creator is all-knowing, all-powerful, in a word, perfect; evil and folly are attributes of a separate being. Coyote, however, rises above—or perhaps has not yet reached—dichotomy. Within this ancient figure the majesty and messiness of the world, the good and the evil, the wise and the foolish, the joyful and the tragic are combined in a complex and intensely creative whole. Captured within these tales, passed down from one generation to the next for thousands upon thousands of years, is the figure of Coyote the all-inclusive, Coyote the incomprehensible, Coyote the ineffable, Coyote the divine, Coyote the holy fool.

X: After the Coming of Whites

long ago brown bears
sang round our lodge fires
tonight they dance
alive through our dreams

William Oandasan,
Yuki

The Arrival of Whites

The year was 1769. Columbus's first voyage nearly three hundred years before was already ancient history. Mexico had been under Spanish rule for well over two centuries. Boston, New York, and Philadelphia were centers of commerce and culture. In Scotland James Watt was working on the steam engine. The modern age was dawning. Yet California was still *terra incognita.* Only a handful of ship captains had touched upon its coast, the interior had never been explored or even penetrated, and prominent landmarks such as San Francisco Bay, the Sacramento River, Mount Shasta, and Yosemite Valley were unknown and unimagined. Not a single non-Indian was living anywhere in California.

In 1769 a small party of Spaniards settled in present-day San Diego. In the next half century *pueblos, ranchos, presidios,* and missions spread along the coast and throughout the coastal valleys as far north as Sonoma County. For the Native Californians the arrival of the Spaniards meant disruption, virtual enslavement, diseases, and death. Wherever the Spaniards settled the native population was decimated, and by 1845 the Indian population of California had fallen from an estimated 310,000 people to 150,000.

The years between 1845 and 1855 brought a flood of Anglos who penetrated into even the most remote valleys and mountains in search of gold, timber, and land. The confrontation between Anglos and Indians was ugly and brutal, and in a mere ten years the Indian population plummeted from 150,000 to 50,000, the result of disease, starvation, and outright murder. Throughout the state native people were immersed in pain, suffering, and annihilation—in an unspeakable, almost inconceivable tragedy.

We had a man at Thomas Creek that had power given to him. He was young. He sang all the time. He drank water and ate once a month. He ate a little of everything, then took one swallow of water and smoked. He stayed in the sweat-house all the time.

Now our captain [chief] used to get out early every morning on top of the sweat-house and, calling everybody by name, would tell them what to do.

This fortuneteller from Thomas Creek would tell the people just how much game they would get and whether any mishaps would fall. He lived across from our present reservation at Paskenta. One day he said, "There are some people from across the ocean who are going to come to this country." He looked for them for three years. "They have some kind of boat [*tco'ltci*] with which they can cross, and they will make it. They are on the way." Finally he said that they were on the land and that they were coming now. He said that they had fire at night and lots to eat. "They cook the same as we do; they smoke after meals, and they have a language of their own. They talk, laugh, and sing, just as we do. Besides, they have five fingers and toes; they are built like we are, only they are light." He said their blood was awfully light.

"They have a four-legged animal which some are riding and some are packing. They haven't any wives, any of them. They all are single. They are bringing some kind of sickness."

So everybody was notified. The night watch and day watch were kept. He said that they had something long which shoots little round things a long distance. They have something short that shoots just the same.

Finally the whites came in at Orland; many of them. When they came in they started shooting. There were thousands of Indians in the hills who went to fighting the whites. The Indians went after them but they couldn't do anything to them. Finally they got to Newville, and the man who was telling these fortunes said the whites were going to be there. The Indians were ready for them. The whites came by Oakes' place and down the flat at one o'clock in the morning. They killed the first Indian that showed himself. The captain told the others to stay in the house and get their bows and arrows ready.

The captain yelled to the whites that he was ready inside the house. He told his men, "When you get ready, run out and crowd into it." The captain sent them to fight at close range. He said, "We are dead anyway." The whites couldn't load their muzzle-loaders, so they used revolvers. The captain told his men to spear them. They fought from morning till afternoon. The Indians had come all the way from Colusa. They killed all those whites. The Indians were afraid of gray horses. They killed the horses. They examined everything. They divided everything up. One old man from south of the Tapscott place took away a lot of their money. His children used to take the money and play with it. Finally he took it up the canyon and hid it. The whites are looking for that money today but can't find it.

Another group of whites came to Mountain House [*lopom*]. They killed many of the Indians. White people hit women and children in the head. One Indian shouted from a rock when the white man started back. The whites came up there, and that Indian went into the rock cave, and they shot one white man from there. But the whites threw fire into the cave and killed all the Indians in there.

They had been hiding in the hills. Indians couldn't get to the salt. They got very weak—they say salt keeps a person fit. There was no rain for three years, and fighting going on every day. No clover, no acorn, juniper berries, or peppergrass. Nothing for three years. Very little rain.

Finally the Indians got smallpox, and the Indian doctor couldn't cure them. They died by the thousands. Gonorrhea came amongst the Indians. That killed a lot of them. My grandfather said that if he had fought he would have been killed too. But he went up to Yolla Bolly Mountain with about six hundred others and stayed three years. On the third winter there was a heavy snowstorm. The snow was over his head. He said women can stand more starvation than men. They singed the hair off a deerhide shoulder strap and ate it.

Men died every day from starvation. That was in Camp of Dark Canyon in the winter. Women would find a little bunch of grass and eat it and would bring a handful back for their husbands. The women would have to chew it for the men. The man was too weak to swallow it. She would take a mouthful of water and pour it into his mouth. That was the way they saved a lot of them.

One man and his brother were lying among the rocks. They wanted to steal something. They saw six riders with forty head of cattle. The Indians lay there and watched them. The riders left

161

after they corralled the cattle. The two Indians got a long willow sprout and made a whip. They tore the fence down and drove the cattle up the creek. They killed one of the steers. First they shot it with an arrow and then hit it in the head with a rock. Then they cut its throat. They skinned it and divided the meat among the people. They had a big feast and they had to make soup for the weak people. They heated water in a basket. Then they put meat in the basket. That saved the people.

After that the whites began to gather up the Indians. They made the Nome Lackee Reservation in Tehama County. They take a tame Indian along when they bring Indians together on a reservation. They worked the Indians on the reservation. Old Martin was given a saddle mule and clothes. He wouldn't wear anything but the shirt—the overalls hurt his legs. He was a kind of foreman. Every Saturday they killed four or five beef and divided it among the Indians. They ground wheat and made biscuits. The women shocked hay. They had to examine all the men and women for disease.

Garland on the present Oakes' place wouldn't let them take the Indians off of his land, and that's what saved them. When they took the Indians to Covelo [in Round Valley, on the Nome Cult Reserve] they drove them like stock. Indians had to carry their own food. Some of the old people began to give out when they got to the hills. They shot the old people who couldn't make the trip. They would shoot children who were getting tired. Finally they got the Indians to Covelo. They killed all who tried to get away and wouldn't return to Covelo.   NOMLAKI

The Massacre at Needle Rock

The Sinkyone were one of several Athapaskan-speaking people who inhabited southern Humboldt County and the extreme northwestern part of Mendocino County. Some fifty Sinkyone villages were spread along the Eel and South Fork of the Eel Rivers, and nearly twenty others dotted the coastal area near present-day Shelter Cove. Before goldrush days the Sinkyone numbered over 4,000 people. By the end of the 1860's they were almost totally wiped out.

Disease contributed to the annihilation. So did starvation, as native people were displaced from their villages, salmon creeks were choked with logging and mining debris, and as fences and property "rights" of white settlers kept native people from hunting, fishing, and gathering in their accustomed places. But a large part of the destruction of the Sinkyone was the result of murder. Supported by a community fearful of the "Indian menace" and greedy for Indian land, legitimized by newspapers that extolled the "manifest destiny" of the white race, groups of men throughout northwestern California formed "volunteer armies" that swooped down upon Indian villages, killing men, women, and children indiscriminately. After such raids the men—often a ragtag group of unemployed miners—would present expense vouchers to the state and federal governments for actions against "hostile Indians." In 1851 and 1852 California authorized over one million dollars for such excursions. It was nothing short of subsidized murder.

My grandfather and all of my family—my mother, my father, and me—were around the house and not hurting anyone. Soon, about ten o'clock in the morning, some white men came. They killed my grandfather and my mother and my father. I saw them do it. I was a big girl at that time. Then they killed my baby sister and cut her heart out and threw it in the brush where I ran and hid. My little sister was a baby, just crawling around. I didn't know what to do. I was so scared that I guess I just hid there a long time with my little sister's heart in my hands. I felt so bad and I was so scared that I just couldn't do anything else. Then I ran into the woods and hid there for a long time. I lived there a long time with a few other people who had got away. We lived on berries and roots and we didn't dare build a fire because the white men might come back after us. So we ate anything we could get. We didn't have clothes after a while, and we had to sleep under logs and in hollow trees because we didn't have anything to cover ourselves with, and it was cold then—in the spring. After a long time, maybe two, three months, I don't know just how long, but sometime in the summer, my brother found me and took me to some white folks who kept me until I was grown and married.

SINKYONE

The Stone and Kelsey Massacre

Under Spanish and Mexican rule the Indians had a place—a miserable place to be sure, but at least there was some accommodation for them in the social and political structure. They were neophytes at the missions, domestics and laborers in the towns, *vaqueros* at the ranches. Spanish soldiers often married Indian women, and their offspring were socially accepted. Indians who adopted Catholic ways might (in theory and sometimes in practice) receive land to farm.

Under the Anglos, however, Indians had no place in the social order, and indeed they were scarcely considered human. Atrocities against the Native Californians were not just the result of a few demented individuals; atrocities were built into the social structure, even written into the laws. Under early California code, for example, an Indian could not bear witness against a white in court; thus whites who entered Indian villages and committed rape, mayhem, and murder could not be prosecuted on the witness of Indians alone. Also, on the statement of any white an Indian could be declared a vagrant and bound over to a white landowner to work for subsistence—in other words, to be a slave. Other laws gave whites custody over Indian minors, leading to an active kidnapping industry wherein youngsters—especially young girls—were stolen from their villages and sold to white farmers and ranchers. All this happened in the 1850's when, it is helpful to remember, slavery was a legal and reputable institution in much of America.

The following narrative describes conditions on a ranch at Clear Lake where Indians were held as virtual slaves by two white men, Andy Kelsey (after whom Kelseyville has been named) and his partner, Stone. In 1849, pushed to desperation by the sadistic treatment they were subjected to, a small group of men rose up and killed both ranchers. A military expedition was sent by the federal government to avenge the killings. According to the official tally sixty Indian people were slaughtered on the island in Clear Lake, another seventy-five were killed along the Russian River.

The narrator, William Ralganal Benson, was born in 1862 and learned about these events directly from those who took part. Having spoken only a Pomo language as a youth and never having attended school, Benson nevertheless taught himself to read and write English. His manuscript is presented here in its entirety—unedited and with his spelling and punctuation preserved.

T he Facts Of Stone and Kelsey Massacre. in Lake County
California. As it was stated to me by the five indians who
went to stone and kelseys house purpose to kill the two
white men. after debateing all night. Shuk and Xasis. these two
men were the instigators of the massacre. it was not because Shuk
and Xasis had any Ill feeling torge the two white men. there were
two indian villages, one on west side and one on the east side. the
indians in both of these camps were starveing. stone or kelsey
would not let them go out hunting or fishing. Shuk and Xasis was
stone and kelsey headriders looking out for stock. cattle horses and
hogs. the horses and cattle were all along the lake on the west side
and some in bachelors valley. also in upper lake. so it took 18
indian herdsman to look after the stock in these places. Shuk and
Xasis was foremans for the herds. and only those herds got
anything to eat. each one of these herders got 4 cups of wheat for a
days work. this cup would hold about one and ahalf pint of water.
the wheat was boiled before it was given to the herders. and the
herders shire with thir famlys. the herders who had large famlys
were also starveing. about 20 old people died during the winter
from starvetion. from severe whipping 4 died. a nephew of an
indian lady who were liveing with stone was shoot to deth by stone.
the mother of this yong man was sick and starveing. this sick
woman told her son to go over to stones wife or the sick womans
sister. tell your aunt that iam starveing and sick tell her that i
would like to have a handfull of wheat. the yong man lost no time
going to stones house. the young man told the aunt what his
mother said. the lady then gave the young man 5 cups of wheat and
tied it up in her apron and the young man started for the camp.
stone came about that time and called the young man back. the
young man stoped stone who was horse back. rode up to the young
man took the wheat from him and then shoot him. the young man
died two days after. such as whipping and tieing thier hands
togather with rope. the rope then thrown over a limb of a tree and
then drawn up untell the indians toes barly touchs the ground and
let them hang there for hours. this was common punishment. when
a father or mother of young girl. was asked to bring the girl to his
house. by stone or kelsey. if this order was not obeyed. he or her

would be whipped or hung by the hands. such punishment occurred two or three times a week. and many of the old men and women died from fear and starvetion.

these two white men had the indians to build a high fence around thir villages. and the head riders were to see that no indian went out side of this fence after dark. if any one was caught out side of this fence after dark was taken to stones and kelseys house and there was tied both hands and feet and placed in a room and kept there all night. the next day was taken to a tree and was tied down. then the strongs man was chosen to whippe the prisoner. the village on the west side was the Qu-Lah-Na-Poh tribes the village on the east side. Xa-Bah-Na-Poh. tribes.

the starvetion of the indians was the cause of the massacre of stone and kelsey. the indians who was starving hired a man by the name of Shuk and a nother man by the name of Xasis. to kill a beef for them. Shuk and Xasis agreed to go out and kill a beef for them. the two men then plan to go out that nigth and kill a beef for them. thir plan then was to take the best horsses in the barn. stones horse which was the best lasso horse. so between the two men. they agreed to take both stones and kelseys horses. so the two men went to stone and kelseys house to see if they had went to bed. it was raining a little. moonligth now and then they found stone and kelsey had went to bed so they went to the barn and took stone and kelseys horses and saddles. Shuk wanted to do the job in the day time but Xasis said stone or kelsey would sure find them and would kill the both of them. Shuk said then somebody is going to get killed on this job. so any how they went out west they knew where a larg band was feeding they soon rounded the band up and Shuk was to make the first lasso Xasis was good on lassing the foot of anox so he was to do the foot lassing. Shuk said to Xasis get redy i see large one hear hurry and come on. Shuk got a chance and threwed the rope on the large ox Xasis came as quick as he could the band began to stampede. the ox also started with the band. the ground was wet and slippery and raining. and before Xasis could get his rope on. Shuks horse fell to the ground. the horse and the

166

ox got away. Xasis tried to lass the horse but could not get near it to throw the rope on. the horse soon found the other horses and it was then much harder to get the horse. so the chase was given up. the two went back to the camp and reported to the peopel who hired them. told them the bad luck they had. Xasis then took the horse he had back to the barn which was kelseys horse. all the men who hired Shuk and Xasis was gathered in Xasiss house. here they debated all night. Shuk and Xasis wanted to kill stone and kelsey. they said stone and kelsey would kill them as soon as they would find out that the horses was taken with out them known; one man got up and suggested that the tribe give stone and kelsey forty sticks of beades which means 16000 beads or 100 dollars. no one agreed. another man suggested that he or Shuk. tell stoneor kelsey that the horse was stolen. no one agreed. and another man suggested that the other horse should be turned out and tell stone and kelsey both horses were stlen. no one agreed. every thing looks bad for Shuk and Xasis. no one agreed with Shuk and Xasis to kill the two white men. at daylight one man agreed to go with Shuk and Xasis. his indian name. Ba-Tus. was known by the whites as Busi. and alittle while later Kra-nas agreed. and as the four men started out another man joind the Shuk and Xasis band: Ma-Laxa-Qe-Tu. while this Debateing was going on the hired or servants boys and girls of stones and kelseys were told by Shuk and Xasis to carrie out allthe guns. bows and arrows. knives and every thing like weapon was taken out of the house by these girls and boys so the two white men was helpless in defense. so Shuk and Xasis knew the white man, did not have any thing to defen themselfs with and they were sure of their victims.

so the five men went to the house where stone and kelsey were liveing. at daylight were to the place where stone always built a fire under a large pot in which he boiled wheat for the indian herders. about 16 of them. these five men waited around this pot untell stone came out to build the fire. Stone came out with pot full of fire which was taken from the fireplace. and said to the indians. whats the matter boys you came Early this morning. some thing rong; the indians said. O nothing me hungry thats all. Qka-Nas: or cayote

Jim as he was known by the whites: Qka-Nas said to the men. I thought you men came to kill this man; give me these arrows and bow. He jerk the bow and the arrows away from Shuk and drew it and as he did Stone rose quickly and turned to Qka-Nas and said what are you trying to do Jim, and as Stone said it. the indian cut loose. the arrow struck the victim pith of the stomach. the victim mediately pull the arrow out and ran for the house. fighting his way. he broke one mans arm with the pot he had. and succeeded in geting in the house and locked the door after him. little later Kelsey came and opened the door and noticed the blood on the doorstep. the indians advanced. Kelsey seen that the indians ment business. he said to them. no matar kelsey. kelsey bueno hombre para vosotros. the indians charged and two of the indians caught kelsey and the fight began. in this fight kelsey was stabed twice in the back. kelsey managed to brake loose. he ran for the creek and the indians after him. a man by the name of Xa-sis or blind Jose as he was known by the whites. who was in pursuit. shot kelsey in the back. kelsey manage to pull the arrow out jest as he got to the creek and jumped in the water and dove under and came out on the other side of the creek. where several indians were waiting. there was one man kelsey knew well. he thought who would save him. this man was Joe sefeis. indian name. Ju-Luh. he beged Joe to save him. Joe he could not save him from being killed. Joe said to kelsey. its too late kelsey; if I attempt to save you. I allso will be killed. I can not save you kelsey; kelsey was geting weak from loss of blood. Big Jim and Joe had kelsey by the arms. Big Jim said to his wife. this is a man who killed our son. take this spear. now you have the chance to take revenge. Big Jim's wife took the spear and stabed the white man in the hart. this womans name was Da-Pi-Tauo. the body was left laying there for the cayotes.

this hapend on the east side of the creek, while this was going on. Xasis and Qra-Nas was trailing the blood up stairs and for a hour allmost. Qra-Nas said they crawled up stairs breathless thinking that stone was yet alive. they opend the door of a wheat bend and saw stones foot Qra-Nas drew his arrow across the bow. redy to cut loose. for a moment they watch the lifeless body. Xa-sis discovered that the body was dead. they then took the body and threw it out the window. and then they called all the people to come and take what wheat and corn they could pack and go to-a hiding place. where they could not be found by the whites. so the indian of both villages came and took all the wheat and corn they could gather in the place. and then went to hide themselfs. some went to Fishels point and somewent to scotts valley. the men went out to kill cattle for their use and every man who was able to ride caught himself a horse. in around the valley and upper lake and bachelor valley. there was about one thousand head of horses and about four thousand head of cattles. so the indians lived fat for a while. Qra-Nas and Ma-Laq-Qe-Tou was chosen to watch the trail that came in from lower lake. and Shuk and Xasis was watching the trail on the west side of the valley. yom-mey-nah and ge-we-leh were watching the trail that came from eight mile valley. two—or three weeks had pass. no white man were seen on eather trail. one day. Qra-nas and ma-Laq-Qe-Tou seen two white men on horse back came over the hill. they stoped on top of the hill. they saw nothing staring around stone and kelseys place. no indians in the village. Qra-nas and Ma-Laq-Qe-Tou . went around behind a small hill to cut the white man off. the white man saw the indians trying to go around behind them. the whites turned and went back before the indians got in back of them. so three or four days went by. no more white man was seen.

one day the lake watchers saw a boat came around the point. som news coming they said to each others. two of the men went to the landing. to see what the news were. they were told that the white warriors had came to kill all the indians around the lake. so hide the best you can. the whites are making boats and with that they are coming up the lake. so we are told by the people down there. so they had two men go up on top of uncle sam mountain. the north peak. from there they watch the lower lake. for three days they watch the lake. one morning they saw a long boat came up the lake with pole on the bow with red cloth. and several of them came. every one of the boats had ten to fifteen men. the smoke signal was given by the two watchmen. every indian around the lake knew the

169

soldiers were coming up the lake. and how many of them. and those who were watching the trail saw the infantrys coming over the hill from lower lake. these two men were watching from ash hill. they went to stones and kelseys house. from there the horsemen went down torge the lake and the soldiers went across the valley torge lakeport. they went on to scotts valley. shoot afew shoots with their big gun and went on to upper lake and camped on Emmerson hill. from there they saw the indian camp on the island. the next morning the white warriors went across in their long dugouts. the indians said they would met them in peace. so when the whites landed the indians went to wellcome them. but the white man was determined to kill them. Ge-We-Lih said he threw up his hands and said no harm me good man. but the white man fired and shoot him in the arm and another shoot came and hit a man staning along side of him and was killed. so they had to run and fight back; as they ran back in the tules and hed under the water; four or five of them gave alittle battle and another man was shoot in the shoulder. some of them jumped in the water and hed in the tuleys. many women and children were killed on around this island. one old lady a (indian) told about what she saw while hiding under abank, in under aover hanging tuleys. she said she saw two white man coming with their guns up in the air and on their guns hung a little girl. they brought it to the creek and threw it in the water. and alittle while later, two more men came in the same manner. this time they had alittle boy on the end of their guns and also threw it in the water. alittle ways from her she, said layed awoman shoot through the shoulder. she held her little baby in her arms. two white men came running torge the woman and baby, they stabed the woman and the baby and, and threw both of them over the bank in to the water. she said she heared the woman say, O my baby; she said when they gathered the dead, they found all the little ones were killed by being stabed, and many of the woman were also killed stabing. she said it took them four or five days to gather up the dead. and the dead were all burnt on the east side the creek. they called it the siland creek. (Ba-Don-Bi-Da-Meh). this old lady also told about the whites hung aman on Emerson siland this indian was met by the soldiers while marching from scotts

170

valley to upper lake. the indian was hung and alarge fire built under the hanging indian. and another indian was caught near Emerson hill. this one was tied to atree and burnt to death.

the next morning the solders started for mendocino county. and there killed many indians. the camp was on the ranch now known as Ed Howell ranch. the solders made camp a little ways below, bout one half mile from the indian camp. the indians wanted to surrender, but the solders did not give them time, the solders went in the camp and shoot them down as tho they were dogs. som of them escaped by going down a little creek leading to the river. and som of them hed in the brush. and those who hed in the brush most of them were killed. and those who hed in the water was over looked. they killed mostly woman and children.

the solders caught two boys age about 14 or 15. the solders took them to lower lake, and then turnd them loose, when the solders started the two boys back, they loded them with meat and hard bread, one said as soon as they got out of site, they threw the meat away and som of the bread also. he said they went on a dog trot for dear life. thinking all the time that the solders would follow them and kill them. he said they would side tract once and awhile and get up on a high peak to see if the solders were coming he said when they got back that night they could nothing but crying. he said all the dead had been taken across to a large dance house had been and was cremated. wetness, Bo-Dom or Jeo Beatti, and Krao Lah, indian name. an old lady said her further dug a large hole in abank of the river and they hed in the hole. one old man said that he was aboy at the time he said the solders shoot his mother, she fell to the ground with her baby in her arms, he said his mother told him to climb high up in the tree, so he did and from there he said he could see the solders runing about the camp and shooting the men and woman and stabing boys and girls. he said mother was not yet dead and was telling him to keep quit. two of the solders heard her talking and ran up to her and stabed her and child. and a little ways from his mother, he said laid a man dieing, holding his boy in his arms the solders also stabed him, but did not

171

kill the boy, they took the boy to the camp, crying, they gave it evry thing they could find in camp but the little boy did not quit crying. it was aboy about three years of age, when the solders were geting redy to move camp, they raped the boy up in ablanket and lief the little boy seting by the fire raped up in a blanket and was stell crying, and that boy is alive today, his name is bill ball, now lives in boonville; One Old man told me about the solders killing the indiuns in this same camp. he said young man from the description he gave. he must have been about 18 or 20 years of age. he said he and another boy about the same age was taken by the soldurs and he said there were two solders in charge of them. one would walk ahead and one behind them. he said the solders took him and the other boy. they both were bearfooted he said when they begin to climb the mountain between mendocino and lake county. he said they were made to keep up with the solders. thir feet were geting sore but they had to keep up with the solders. when they were climbing over the bottlerock mountain.thir feet were cutup by the rocks and thir feet were bleeding and they could not walk up with the solders. the man behind would jab them with the sharp knife fixed on the end of the gun. he said one of the solders came and looked at thir feet and went to abox opened it took acup and diped something out of asack and brought it to them and told them both of them to hold their foots on a log near by. the solder took ahand full of the stuff and rubed it in the cuts on the bottom of thir feet. he said he noticed that the stuff the solder put on their feet look like salt. sure enough it was salt. the solder tied clouth over their feet and told them not to take them off. he said the tears were roling down his cheeks. he said all the solders came and stood around them laughing. he said they roled and twested for about two hours. and they also rubed salt in the wounds on their seats and backs wher they jabed them with the solders big knife. as he call it. two or three days later the chife solder told them they could go back. they was then gaven meat and bread, all they could pack. he said they started on thir back journey. he said it was all most difficult for them to walk but raped alot of cloth around thir feet and by doing so made thir way all right. he said the meat and bread got too heavy for fast traveling so they threw the meat and some of the bread away. looking back all the time thinking that the solders would follow them and kill them. now and then they would side tract. and look back to see if the solders were following them. after seen no solders following them they would start out for another run. he said they traveled in such manner untell they got to thir home. he said to himself. hear Iam not to see my mother and sister but to see thir blood scattered over the ground like water and thir bodys for coyotes to devour. he said he sat down under a tree and cryed all day.   POMO

I No Longer Believe

In 1864 the Modoc were pushed off their land and moved northward to a reservation in Oregon, where they were forced to live side-by-side with their ancestral enemies, the Klamath. Tensions were high and the Modoc wretched, when in 1870 a subchief named Kintpuash—known to whites as Captain Jack—murdered a Klamath shaman and fled, taking with him fifty-three warriors and many women, children, and old people. The band traveled south and hid itself among the caves and jagged outcroppings of the lava bed region near Tule Lake, where for six months they fended off a force of over 1,000 soldiers. The tragic, dramatic, sordid conflict, marked by barbarities and betrayals, became known as the "Modoc War." In the end Captain Jack was captured and hanged, and the Modoc people were dispersed, some remaining on the Klamath Reservation, others being exiled to Oklahoma.

The following narrative touches upon the Modoc War and suggests its cultural aftermath. As everywhere in California, native values were crumbling beneath the onslaught of whites. Overnight elaborate interlocking systems of belief, technology, and social organization were rendered invalid. A massive death rate shattered the familial, tribal, and ceremonial affinities that bound people together and gave them their very identity. Property and territorial rights—developed and sustained for hundreds of years—were instantly swept aside in arbitrary land grabs and treaties. The sinew-backed bow—strong, flexible, polished, and painted—seemed a pitiful toy compared with the rifle; a basket labored over for weeks was less durable than a cheap tin pail; the harpoon, fishing weir, and even the ancient salmon chants were useless in streams choked with mining and logging debris. New diseases and agents of death made

173

the shamans look like doddering, helpless old men and women. Traditional wisdom that stressed co-operation, moderation, and fitting in seemed
outmoded in a frontier society which demanded individual initiative and
encouraged competition. Although many people hung onto traditional
values and beliefs—and indeed there are many who still do—for others
the white invasion brought about a cultural as well as a physical collapse.
Sadly and achingly, even people of good family and traditional upbringing
turned their backs on the beliefs of their people.

In ancient times described in myths the doctors really cured
people, but now they just fool them. When I was old enough to
remember, my father and another chief wanted a doctor to kill
a man forty miles away. The doctor agreed. But I know for sure
that he didn't even kill that man. Even when a doctor tries to kill a
man living nearby he always fails. But when someone does die the
doctor wants all the credit and claims that he killed the man.

During the Modoc War the strongest doctor was supposed to be
Curly-headed Doctor. He took a long cord and painted it red and
put it around the whole camp. He said that the federal soldiers
would fall down and die if they touched the string; they would
never be able to cross it. The people believed him and danced with
him all night, singing all the while.

A few days later we saw soldiers coming toward our camp. As
they came closer we saw that one of the leaders had a sabre. Behind him two other leaders were followed by the troops. As they
came close to the string the leaders shouted, "Mark;" the soldiers
dropped to their knees. They shouted, "Fire," and the soldiers
shot all around. They then ran over the string. The string did not
kill the soldiers; Indian bullets did that. I saw it with my own eyes.
After that I didn't believe any more.

The doctor claims he can make rain. He can make the strongest
wind, too. He can make heavy snow. He can stop wind, rain, or
snow. My father once asked a doctor to stop a bad storm. The
doctor agreed. But with all his singing and dancing for two nights
the storm didn't cease. Sometimes a doctor will sing and dance for
five nights and still the bad weather continues. The people are disappointed that the doctor can't change the weather. But they try to
believe him, and they try again sometime. Even though they know

174

the doctor can't make it rain or snow they still believe in him. If the rain comes in two or three days, the doctor says that he brought it. If the storm stops, the doctor says that he did it, and everyone believes him. As far as I can remember a doctor never stopped rain or wind.

My father, John Sconchin, was an intelligent man. The last time my father believed in doctors was when the soldiers crossed the string. He said, "This is the last time that we will believe in doctors. We'll ask them no more." Then my father and the others discussed the many times they had asked doctors to kill other people and it never happened; how many times they called doctors to cure and they didn't cure; and how many times they asked for rain and didn't get it. They spoke of how the doctors always claimed they were responsible when these things did happen. My father and the others were badly disappointed in the doctors.

But most people still believe. MODOC

Four Dream Cult Songs

Beginning in 1870 a series of native messianic movements swept through California. These movements transformed beliefs, gave hope—or at least escape—to a defeated people, and reshaped and revitalized a deeply shaken religious faith. The so-called Ghost Dance cult originated among the Paviotso of Walker Lake, Nevada, and spread westward with unbelievable rapidity. Native "prophets" carried the word from village to village: Indian people must gather together and dance for days on end, after which the ghosts of Indian dead would march back into the world, drive out the whites, and usher in a new age.

As the cult was transmitted from one tribal group to another variations developed. The Earth Lodge cult preached that the end of the world was imminent and that only native people who secluded themselves in traditional earth lodges and performed proper rituals would survive the impending Armageddon.

The Bole-Maru cult, which developed out of the Earth Lodge cult, abandoned doctrines of world destruction and the return of the dead, stressing instead ideas of the afterlife, a Supreme Being, and the importance of dreaming. The Bole-Maru was especially important among the

175

Patwin and Pomo. It helped refocus and invigorate native shamanism (its effects are still felt among shamans practicing today), and it served as a link between traditional belief systems and the Pentecostal Christianity which would provide a backdoor entry for many Indians into the white world and the white way of thinking.

Among the Wintu a local Dream Dance cult emerged in 1872, an apparent outgrowth of the Bole-Maru, and lasted some forty years. A cult dreamer would meet a dead friend or relative in a dream and receive a song. The next day the dreamer sang the song publicly and danced to it, often with elaborate costume and ritual. Afterwards the song became the common property of all who heard it, and anyone might sing it at future Dream Dance rituals.

The songs that individual dreamers received from dead friends and relatives were often hauntingly beautiful.

I.

Down west, down west we dance,
    We spirits dance.
Down west, down west we dance,
    We spirits dance.
Down west, down west we dance,
    We spirits weeping dance,
    We spirits dance.

II.

There above, there above,
    At the mystical earthlodge of the south,
    Spirits are wafted along the roof and fall.
There above, there above,
    At the mystical earthlodge of the south,
    Spirits are wafted along the roof and fall.
There above, there above,
    Spirits are wafted along the roof and fall,
    Flowers bend heavily on their stems.

III.

It is above that you and I shall go;
    Along the Milky Way you and I shall go;
It is above that you and I shall go;
    Along the Milky Way you and I shall go;
It is above that you and I shall go;
Along the flower trail you and I shall go;
    Picking flowers on our way you and I shall go.

IV.

Above where the minnow maiden sleeps at rest
    The flowers droop,
    The flowers rise again.
Above where the minnow maiden sleeps at rest
    The flowers droop,
    The flowers rise again.
Above where the minnow maiden sleeps at rest
    The flowers droop,
    The flowers rise again.   WINTU

A Fishing Experience

The Kashaya, one of the seven linguistic divisions of the Pomo, lived along the coast of Sonoma County. Their first major white contact was with Fort Ross, the Russian outpost founded in 1812. Unlike the Spaniards who forced the Indians into missions, or the Anglos who stole the land and treated the native residents as trespassers, the Russians came merely to hunt sea otter and grow grain for their Alaskan colony. Their behavior toward the Indians was relatively indifferent, even benign. By the time the Russians deserted Fort Ross in 1842 the Kashaya, who had often traded and worked there for wages, had become gradually acclimated to white ways. Thus their subsequent clash with Mexican and Anglo settlers—while harsh—was not totally devastating. Also, since the

177

Sonoma coast offered few harbors, no gold, and poor agriculture, it was settled more sparsely than much of the rest of California.

By the 1870's a white rancher, Charlie Haupt, had married a Kashaya woman, and it was on his sprawling property that many Kashaya people found refuge. Here two villages grew, one of them the *Abaloneville* mentioned in the following narrative.

From the late nineteenth century to the present the Kashaya have remained relatively secluded and even aloof, greatly influenced by the isolationist policies of certain spiritual leaders who rose up among them. Perhaps the most influential of these leaders was Annie Jarvis, whose presence dominated the Kashaya from 1912 to 1943. She forbade gambling and drinking, banned marriage with the whites, kept the children out of boarding schools, and encouraged the use of the Kashaya language and the retention of many traditional customs. After Annie Jarvis, Essie Parrish, a shaman, held sway until her death in 1979.

Because of their unusual history the Kashaya have survived far better—in terms of both culture and population—than any other Central California people. Originally one of the smallest of the Pomo divisions, numbering no more than 600 to 800 people, today (while greatly diminished) they are the largest. Over 150 people identify themselves as Kashaya, the language is still actively spoken by several dozen, and the social and ceremonial life retains many traditional elements.

While the Kashaya escaped annihilation, the immense decline in population indicates that they too underwent great suffering. As ranching and logging cut people off from their hunting and gathering grounds, the Kashaya became more and more dependent upon farm work and day labor. Living on the fringes of white society they often found themselves starving in what had once been a land of plenty.

I am going to tell about something we did while living in Abaloneville—going fishing and hunting for food to eat. At the time white food wasn't plentiful—in my youth. We made harpoons. I too knew how to do that. We fastened three nails together and sharpened the one in the middle on the point. Where the two side nails were fastened we called "ears." The harpoon head was then wrapped with cord, smeared with pitch, and smoothed off with a hot rock. A cord was attached to the head and tied onto a pole. That's how we carried it around to spear fish with. We Indians called the harpoon *napa*.

Now I am going to tell how we used to go fishing. We walked a long way to the fish. One time, when we had arisen early in the morning, we set out without much food—without any food except what we had already eaten that morning. Then we went a long way. We went a long way downhill; going downhill was good because we didn't get tired. When we reached the water, we walked upstream. "Upstream is the only way to search for fish," the old time people had said when teaching us. We do the same thing too; if we went downstream the fish would get our scent as we waded across the water. That is why the people of long ago said to go only upstream to fish. We, too, did it that way. We walked along and walked along towards what we call *ahsahq-a* [fish holes], where the fish lie together.

When we had got close to that pool, we looked into the water. One person counted and said, "Sixty fish are gathered." Then we got our poles ready, fastened on the harpoon points, and stabbed. We speared for a long time. All day we worked the fish there. I suppose a few fish were left, but we speared almost all. There must have been sixty fish lying there.

Then we all quit. We were completely soaked; even our bodies, our entire bodies, were soaked. We came up out of the water. We divided the fish up according to how many each could carry. I suppose there were six or seven given to each person, for there were ten of us carrying. Filling our sacks we slung them over our backs and went upwards along the trail that we had come down.

A few people grew tired and weak from hunger. Then they got so that they couldn't move their feet, they had grown so weary. I felt the same way too. Whenever I sat down I just keeled over to sleep and felt completely unable to get up. We walked along that way. That happened to many men—they were sleeping, unable to get up. I was just barely moving along myself—getting up, starting off, walking along. Only a few of us reached the summit. The rest were still being weak from hunger. I felt the same way too, getting terribly weak. Whenever we sat down we went to sleep and didn't feel like getting up. And packing those heavy fish, too, made it even worse. Only a few of us reached home. When we arrived home we were worn out. All the strength that we had felt in us earlier was gone—only a little, just enough to move our legs was left.

When we had arrived home, we explained. "The other men are still resting along the trail, unable to walk, weak from hunger," we said. The other men packed some food and clothes and departed, looking for them. When they had eaten the food and put on the dry clothes, they began to feel better. Before the searchers had left and found them, we had told them where, on which trail, we had gone to the river, so that the men would be found easily. They also found the fish they had been carrying. When they had been fed they became much stronger, and, picking up their fish, they returned.

That is how we used to do things—help one another. If someone should fail somewhere in the wilderness, we would go after him. When he had been strengthened, he would be led home. Even if that happened at night, we would still go.

This that I have told is a true story about what I saw myself. This is the end.   POMO

I Am the Last

Death and destruction continued throughout the nineteenth century at a horrendous rate. In 1769 there were an estimated 310,000 native people in California; in 1845, 150,000; in 1855, 50,000; in 1900, fewer than 20,000.

The fate of the Chunut, Wowol, and Tachi—three Yokuts groups who lived around the shores of Tulare Lake in the San Joaquin Valley—is typical. They once numbered about 6,500 people, but even by 1850 disease and conquest reduced them to about 1,100. Then came the steady flow of white settlers into the Central Valley. Tribal groups were uprooted and forced onto barren reservations without adequate food or shelter. Eventually economic necessity—more bluntly, desperation—drove people from the reservations into nearby farms, ranches, and cities to seek whatever work they could find. As the older people died, the younger people scattered and intermarried with strangers. In 1933 an eighty-five year old Chunut woman named Yoimut lamented the extinction of her people.

I am the last full-blood Chunut left. My children are part Spanish. I am the only one who knows the whole Chunut or Wowol language. When I am gone no one will have it. I have to be the last one. All my life I want back our good old home on Tulare Lake. But I guess I can never have it. I am a very old Chunut now and I guess I can never see the old days again.

Now my daughter and her Mexican husband work in the cotton fields around Tulare and Waukena. Cotton, cotton, cotton, that is all that is left. Chunuts cannot live on cotton. They cannot sing their old songs and tell their old stories where there is nothing but cotton. My children feel foolish when I sing my songs. But I sing anyway:

Toke-uh lih-nuh Wa-tin-hin nah yo
Hiyo-umne ahe oonook miuh-wah.

That is all.

YOKUTS

I Remember

Native Californians alive today grew up in a predominantly white world. Almost all speak English as a native language. Their memories, nevertheless, still resound with echoes of a deeply-felt past, as in this poem by Edward Montez.

I remember the scent of acorn soup cooking and deer meat frying
    in quiet evenings of summer.
And shivering under thin blankets in winter and watching the wall
    paper dance to the force of the winter winds outside.
I remember the cry of an owl in the night and I knew it was an
    ominous warning, a cry of death.
I remember running in the dust behind the medicine truck when it
    came to the reservation, lifesavers was a free treat.
And grandpa sitting in his favorite resting chair under his favorite
    shade tree with his dog "Oly" by his side.
I remember running naked and screaming with my aunt in hot
    pursuit, a stick in her hand, she always caught me.

181

And every summer we would swim in the river and let the sun bake
    us until we were a shade less than purple, basking on the
    river bank, undisturbed, at peace.
And I remember grandma toiling in the beanfields while I played
    with my army truck on the fender of a "49" Plymouth.
I remember going to the movies in town on Saturday nights with
    fifty cents in my pocket, thirty-five cents for the ticket and the
    rest was mine.
Eating popcorn and drinking water from a discarded coke cup and
    rooting for the Indians to win, and they never did, but that was
    yesterday.   WINTU-SHOSHONE

For the White Poets

Indian culture is still alive in California. Since the turn of the century the
native population has increased dramatically. Some two dozen native
languages are still being spoken, many traditional attitudes and values
are still being passed on from one generation to the next. After years of
submergence Native Californians are regaining a sense of self-respect
and pride in their own past; many are learning once again the arts of
basketry and dance. Today Native Californians are writing texts and tribal
histories, and they are painfully facing up to the momentousness of the
crimes committed against them.

Also the last decade has seen an interest—even a fascination—by
whites in Indian ways. Whites flock to Indian reservations, museums,
trading posts, and to the acorn dances and "big-times" still held in the
Sierra. Indian basketmakers have a following of whites learning the
ancient craft; people read (and write) ever-increasing numbers of books
on Indians. Is this just another form of exploitation? After robbing people
of life, land, language, and culture, have we whites now returned to pluck
from them bits of wisdom, philosophy, and poetry with which to ornament
our lives? Or can our culture integrate ancient wisdom and values in any
significant way? It is fitting to end this book with an uncomfortable yet
necessary challenge by poet, Wendy Rose.

For the white poets who would be Indian
just once. Just long enough
to snap up the words
fishhooked from our tongues;
you think of us now
when you kneel on the earth,
when you turn holy
in a temporary tourism
of our souls.

With words
you paint your faces,
chew your doeskin, touch breast
and tree as if
sharing a mother were
all it takes, could bring
instant and primal knowledge.

You think of us only when
your voice wants for roots,
when you have sat back on
your heels and become
primitive.

You finish your poems
and go back.   MIWOK-HOPI

Photographs

ABOVE: Doorway of a Yurok house. *Courtesy of Calif. Dept. of Parks and Recreation.*

RIGHT: Fanny Flounder, the Yurok shaman described in "A Doctor Acquires Power" (page 93). *Courtesy of Humboldt State Coll. Library.*

OPPOSITE PAGE: Yurok woman (Elsie Frank) in traditional dress. *Courtesy of Lowie Museum of Anthropology.*

PRECEDING PAGE: Robert Spott, Yurok, narrator of "The Osegen Slave" (page 41) and "A Doctor Acquires Power" (page 93). *Courtesy of Calif. Dept. of Parks and Recreation.*

OPPOSITE PAGE: Captain John, a Hupa leader. (See page 61.) *Courtesy of Humboldt State College Library.*

LEFT: Yurok village with sweathouse in the foreground. *Courtesy of Calif. Dept. of Parks and Recreation.*

BELOW: McCann, narrator of the Hupa story about the moon (page 76), measuring a string of dentalia against money marks tattooed on his forearm. *Courtesy of Calif. Dept of Parks and Recreation.*

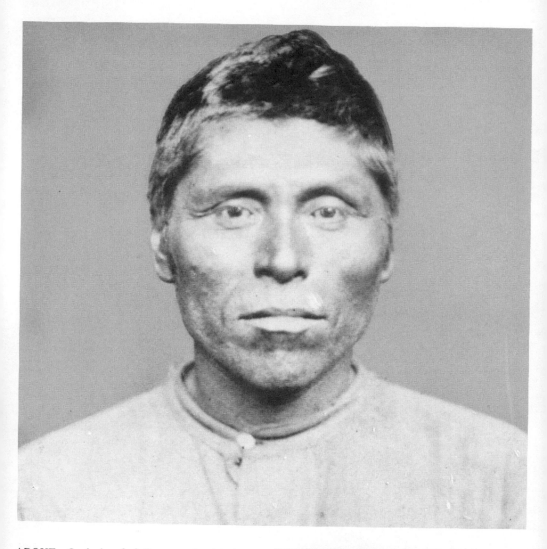

ABOVE: Curly-headed Doctor, the Modoc shaman who failed to stop the advance of U.S. soldiers in the Modoc War (page 174). *Courtesy of the Bancroft Library.*

RIGHT: John Sconchin, Captain Jack's assistant in the Modoc War (page 174). *Courtesy of Calif. Dept. of Parks and Recreation.*

OPPOSITE PAGE: A Karok man dressed for battle. *Courtesy of the Smithsonian Institution.*

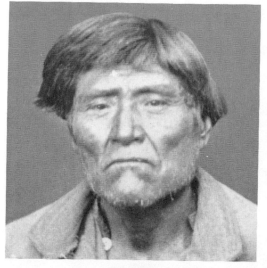

ABOVE: A Yuki man in dance regalia. *Courtesy of Lowie Museum of Anthropology.*

TOP LEFT: Jerry James, Wiyot, narrator of the Pleiades story (page 75). *Courtesy of the Bancroft Library.*

LEFT: Sally Bell, Sinkyone, who recounted the Needle Rock Massacre (page 162). *Courtesy of the Bancroft Library.*

OPPOSITE PAGE: A Wintu earth lodge with sacred pole and a feather-cloaked dancer during the Hesi ceremony (page 48). *Courtesy of Lowie Museum of Anthropology.*

ABOVE: A Pomo tule house in the Clear Lake area. *Courtesy of the Bancroft Library.*

RIGHT: William Ralganal Benson, Pomo, who narrated "The Stone and Kelsey Massacre" (page 164) and the Pomo creation epic (page 123). *Courtesy of Lowie Museum of Anthropology.*

OPPOSITE PAGE: Pomo man in dance costume with a bird-bone whistle in his mouth. *Courtesy of Lowie Museum of Anthropology.*

ABOVE: A Sierra Miwok dance house. *Courtesy of Lowie Museum of Anthropology.*

LEFT: Yoimut, the last of the Chunut Yokuts (page 180). *Courtesy of Mr. Frank F. Latta.*

OPPOSITE PAGE: Tom Williams, a Sierra Miwok. He was a village headman and narrator of three selections (pages 37, 100, and 107). *Courtesy of Lowie Museum of Anthropology.*

TOP: Cahuilla house in the desert. *Courtesy of the Smithsonian Institution Libraries, Special Collections.*

ABOVE: Luiseño sweat-house. *Courtesy of the Calif. Historical Society.*

OPPOSITE PAGE: Two Mohave women. *Courtesy of the Bancroft Library.*

ABOVE: A Tipai-Ipai shaman in dance costume. *Courtesy of Lowie Museum of Anthropology.*

Footnotes

Page 9. LIVELY, LIVELY. From *Music of the Maidu Indians of California* by Frances Densmore. Los Angeles: Southwest Museum. 1958. Page 20. This song, a "duck dance song," was collected in Chico in 1937 from a Maidu woman named Mrs. Amanda Wilson, then in her seventies.

Page 11. THE CRADLE. From "Nomlaki Ethnography" by Walter Goldschmidt. *University of California Publications in American Archaeology and Ethnology,* Vol 42 (4). Berkeley. 1951. Page 371. Narrated by Jeff Jones, a Nomlaki, in 1936. Jones was then about seventy years old. A photograph taken at the time shows him to have been a strikingly handsome and intelligent-looking man, with great drooping moustachios and laughing eyes.

Page 12. MY GRANDFATHER. From *Autobiographies of Three Pomo Women* by Elizabeth Colson. Archaeological Research Facility, Department of Anthropology, University of California at Berkeley. 1974. Page 129. The narrator, whose name is not revealed, was born in 1882 and dictated her reminiscences in 1941.

Page 13. LEARNING TO HUNT. From "South Diegueño Customs" by Leslie Spier. *University of California Publications in American Archaeology and Ethnology,* Vol 20. Berkeley. 1923. Page 336. The reminiscence was dictated in 1920 near present-day Campo in San Diego County by a man named Jim McCarthy, then over eighty years old.

Page 15. A MAN WITHOUT FAMILY. From *Deep Valley* by Burt and Ethel Aginsky. New York: Stein and Day. 1967. Page 18. The statement was narrated in 1935 by a man who was reputed to have been 112 years old.

Page 16. PUBERTY DANCE SONG. From *Tribes of California* by Stephen Powers. Washington: U.S. Government Printing Office. 1877. Page 236. The song was recorded by Powers in 1871 or 1872.

Page 17. ROLLING HEAD. From "Wintu Myths" by Cora Du Bois and Dorothy Demetracopoulou. *University of California Publications in American Archaeology and Ethnology,* Vol 28. Berkeley. 1931. Page 362. Told by Syke Mitchell of the McCloud branch of the Wintu in 1929.

Page 19. SAND PAINTING SERMON. From *Handbook of the Indians of California* by Alfred Kroeber. Washington: U.S. Government Printing Office. 1925. Page 684.

Page 21. INITIATION INTO THE GHOST SOCIETY. From *Handbook of the Indians of California* by Alfred Kroeber. Washington: U.S. Government Printing Office. 1925. Page 188.

Page 23. I AM A FINE-LOOKING WOMAN. From *Music of the Maidu Indians of California* by Frances Densmore. Los Angeles: Southwest Museum. 1958. Page 50. The song was recorded in 1937 from a Maidu woman named Amanda Wilson. (See footnote for page 9, "Lively, Lively.")

Page 25. HOW THE WOMAN GOT EVEN. From "Karuk Indian Myths" by John Harrington. *Bureau of American Ethnology Bulletin* 107. Washington. 1932. Page 12. Narrated by a sixty-five year old Karok woman, Phoebe Maddux, whose Indian name, Imkanvan, meant "Wild-sunflower-greens-gatherer."

Page 28. THREE LOVE SONGS. From "Wintu Songs" by Dorothy Demetracopoulou. *Anthropos*, Vol 30. 1935. Page 492. The first two songs were sung by a man named Harry Marsh, the third sung by Fanny Brown.

Page 29. THE HANDSOME MAN. From "Wintu Myths" by Cora Du Bois and Dorothy Demetracopoulou. *University of California Publications in American Archaeology and Ethnology*, Vol 28. Berkeley. 1931. Page 326. Told by Jenny Curl of the McCloud branch of the Wintu in 1929.

Page 32. FOOTBALL FREE- FOR-ALL. From "Nisenan Texts and Dictionary" by Hans Uldall and William Shipley. *University of California Publications in Linguistics*, Vol 46. Berkeley. 1966. Page 91. A reminiscence collected in 1930 or 1931, most likely from a Nisenan man named William Joseph of Auburn, who at the time was about seventy-five years old.

Page 33. THE TOLOWIM-WOMAN AND BUTTERFLY MAN. From "Maidu Myths" by Roland Dixon. *Bulletin of the American Museum of Natural History*, Vol 17. New York. 1902. Page 95.

Page 35. WOMEN ARE TROUBLEMAKERS. From "Nomlaki Ethnography" by Walter Goldschmidt. *University of California Publications in American Archaeology and Ethnology*, Vol 42 (4). Berkeley. 1951. Page 370. Narrator was Jeff Jones. (See footnote for page 11, "The Cradle.")

Page 37. THE YOUNG CHIEF. From "Central Miwok Ceremonies" by Edward W. Gifford. *University of California Anthropological Records*, Vol 14 (4). Berkeley. 1955. Page 262. This speech was transcribed and translated from a phonograph recording made by a man named Molestu (Tom Williams), chief of the Central Miwok village of Chakachino in Tuolumne County. Williams was over eighty years old when the recording was made, some time in the second or third decade of the present century.

Page 39. TARANTULA. From "Coast Yuki Myths" by Edward W. Gifford. *Journal of American Folklore*, Vol 50. 1937. Page 170.

Page 41. THE OSEGEN SLAVE AT ESPEU. From "Yurok Narratives" by Robert Spott and Alfred Kroeber. *University of California Publications in American Archaeology and Ethnology*, Vol 35. Berkeley. 1942. Page 152. Robert Spott, born in 1888, dictated this and other narratives between the years 1933 and 1940 to Alfred Kroeber. Kroeber was struck with Spott's excellent memory, his intellectual inclinations, and his "extraordinary sensitivity to the value of native culture."

Page 44. PROPERTY. From "Nomlaki Ethnography" by Walter Goldschmidt. *University of California Publications in American Archaeology and Ethnology*, Vol 42 (4). Berkeley. 1951. Page 333. Narrated by Jeff Jones. (See footnote for page 11, The Cradle.")

Page 45. CHOOSING A CHIEF. From "Ethnography of the Yuma Indians" by C. Darryl Forde. *University of California Publications in American Archaeology and Ethnology*, Vol 28. Berkeley. 1931. Page 135. The account was given by a Yuma man named Patrick Miguel in 1929. Miguel was in his early fifties at the time.

Page 47. MESSENGERS. From "Nomlaki Ethnography" by Walter Goldschmidt. *University of California Publications in American Archaeology and Ethnology*, Vol 42 (4). Berkeley. 1951. Page 342. Narrated by Jeff Jones. (See footnote for page 11, "The Cradle.")

Page 48. FEAST ORATION. From "Wintun Hesi Ceremony" by Samuel Barrett. *University of California Publications in American Archaeology and Ethnology*, Vol 14. Berkeley. 1919. Page 461. The speech was originally recorded in 1906.

Page 50. FOOTBALL BIG-TIME. From "Nisenan Texts and Dictionary" by Hans Uldall and William Shipley. *University of California Publications in Linguistics*, Vol 46. Berkeley. 1966. Page 91. A reminiscence most likely of William Joseph. (See footnote for page 32, "Football Free-For-All.")

Page 51. WARFARE. From "Nomlaki Ethnography" by Walter Goldschmidt. *University of California Publications in American Archaeology and Ethnology*, Vol 42 (4). Berkeley. 1951. Page 341. Narrated by Jeff Jones. (See footnote for page 11, "The Cradle.")

Page 53. GREAT HORNED OWLS. From "Kashaya Texts" by Robert Oswalt. *University of California Publications in Linguistics*, Vol 36. Berkeley. 1964. Page 163. The story was collected in 1958 from Herman James, then nearly eighty years old. An accomplished storyteller, James learned this and other tales from his maternal grandmother who was born some eight years before the Russians settled at Fort Ross in 1812.

Page 55. BUILDING A DANCE HOUSE. From "Nomlaki Ethnography" by Walter Goldschmidt. *University of California Publications in American Archaeology and Ethnology*, Vol 42 (4). Berkeley. 1951. Page 422. Narrated by Jeff Jones. (See footnote for page 11, "The Cradle.")

Page 59. AT THE TIME OF DEATH. From "The Religion of the Luiseño and Diegueño Indians of Southern California" by Constance Du Bois. *University of California Publications in American Archaeology and Ethnology*, Vol 8 (3). Berkeley. 1908. Page 110. Recorded soon after the turn of the century from an elderly man named José Albañas.

Page 61. THE MEN I KNEW. From "Personality Variation in a Primitive Society" by William Wallace. *Journal of Personality*, Vol 15. 1947. Page 321.

Page 64. OLD GAMBLER'S SONG. From *Tribes of California* by Stephen Powers. Washington: U.S. Government Printing Office. 1877. Page 308. Collected in the early 1870's.

Page 64. GRANDFATHER'S PRAYER. From "Some Indian Texts Dealing With The Supernatural" by Dorothy Demetracopoulou Lee. *Review of Religion*, Vol 5. 1941. Page 407. The prayer was recalled by a granddaughter, Sadie Marsh.

Page 66. CRYING. From *Autobiographies of Three Pomo Women* by Elizabeth Colson. Archaeological Research Facility, Department of Anthropology, University of California at Berkeley. 1974. Page 116. The anonymous narrator was born in 1882 and dictated her reminiscences in 1941.

Page 66. DEATH SONG. From *Mulu'wetam: The First People; Cupeño Oral History and Language* by Jane Hill and Rosinda Nolasquez. Banning, Calif.: Malki Museum Press. 1973. Page 78a.

Page 67. BURIAL ORATION. From "Wintu Ethnography" by Cora Du Bois. *University of California Publications in American Archaeology and Ethnology*, Vol 36. Berkeley. 1935. Page 79.

Page 68. THE LAND OF THE DEAD. From "Serrano Tales" by Ruth Benedict. *Journal of American Folklore*, Vol 39. 1926. Page 8. The story was told by a woman named Rosa Marongo.

Page 69. SUMMONS TO A MOURNING CEREMONY. From "Central Miwok Ceremonies" by Edward Gifford. *University of California Anthropological Records*, Vol 14. Berkeley. 1955. Page 263. This speech was collected at Bald Rock in 1913 from a man known as Chief Yanapayak.

Page 73. PLANTS ARE THOUGHT TO BE ALIVE. From "Pomo Folkways" by Edwin Loeb. *University of California Publications in American Archaeology and Ethnology*, Vol 19 (2). Berkeley. 1926. Page 149. For information about the narrator, William Ralganal Benson, see the footnote for page 123, "Marumda and Kuksu Make the World."

Page 75. THE PLEIADES AND THEIR PURSUER. From *The North American Indian*, Vol 13, by Edward Curtis. Norwood, Mass.: Plimpton Press. 1924. Page 196. The story, collected by the photographer Edward Curtis, was narrated by a man named Jerry James, born in 1859.

Page 76. THE LUNAR ECLIPSE. From "Hupa Texts" by Pliny Goddard. *University of California Publications in American Archaeology and Ethnology*, Vol 1 (2). Berkeley. 1904. Page 196. The story was told at the turn of the century by a man known as McCann. He was described as being white-haired, perhaps seventy or seventy-five years old. (Like other Native Californians born before the coming of whites, he did not know his exact age.)

Page 77. SUN AND MOON. From "Maidu Myths" by Roland Dixon. *Bulletin of the American Museum of Natural History*, Vol 17. New York. 1902. Page 78.

Page 78. THE GREEDY FATHER. From "The Karok Language" by William Bright. *University of California Publications in Linguistics*, Vol 13. Berkeley. 1957. Page 215. The narrator was Lottie Beck of modern-day Orleans who told the story in the early 1950's.

Page 80. THE STICK HUSBAND. From "Coast Yuki Myths" by Edward Gifford. *Journal of American Folklore*, Vol 50. 1937. Page 168.

Page 82. THE GIRL WHO MARRIED RATTLESNAKE. From "Pomo Myths" by Samuel Barrett. *Bulletin of the Public Museum of the City of Milwaukee*, Vol 15. Milwaukee, Wisc. 1933. Page 373. The story was told soon after the turn of the century by a man named Charley Brown. Brown spoke the northern Pomo language, which before the coming of whites was used from present-day Ukiah and Willets west to the coast.

Page 83. THE MAN AND THE OWLS. From "Myths of South Central California" by Alfred Kroeber. *University of California Publications in American Archaeology and Ethnology*, Vol 4 (4). Berkeley. 1907. Page 228. The story was collected from an anonymous storyteller of the Yawdanchi Yokuts tribal group which inhabited the Tule River drainage in the foothills northeast of present-day Bakersfield.

Page 85. INITIATION SONG. From *Handbook of the Indians of California* by Alfred Kroeber. Washington: U.S. Government Printing Office. 1925. Page 194.

Page 85. PRAYER FOR GOOD FORTUNE. From *Handbook of the Indians of California* by Alfred Kroeber. Washington: U.S. Government Printing Office. 1925. Page 511. Recorded from the Yawelmani Yokuts group of the Kern River area.

Page 87. TO THE EDGE OF THE EARTH. From "Wintu Songs" by Dorothy Demetracopoulou. *Anthropos*, Vol 30. 1935. Page 488. The song was recorded in 1929 from a woman named Fanny Brown.

Page 89. MY MOUNTAIN. From "Two Paiute Autobiographies" by Julian Steward. *University of California Publications in American Archaeology and Ethnology*, Vol 33. Berkeley. 1934. Page 423. This selection was excerpted from a longer work narrated by a Paiute man named Jack Stewart in 1927 or 1928. Stewart, whose Indian name was Hoavadunaki, was nearly a hundred years old at the time and had already reached maturity when the whites first settled in Owens Valley in 1861.

Page 92. THE LONG SNAKE. From "Karuk Indian Myths" by John Harrington. *Bureau of American Ethnology Bulletin* 107. Washington. 1932. Page 9. Narrated by a sixty-five year old woman, Phoebe Maddux. (See footnote for page 25, "How the Woman Got Even.")

Page 93. A DOCTOR ACQUIRES POWER. From "Yurok Narratives" by Robert Spott and Alfred Kroeber. *University of California Publications in American Archaeology and Ethnology*, Vol 35. Berkeley. 1942. Page 158. For more information on the narrator, Robert Spott, see footnote for page 41, "The Osegen Slave at Espeu."

Page 96. HOW I GOT MY POWERS. From *Handbook of the Indians of California* by Alfred Kroeber. Washington: U.S. Government Printing Office. 1925. Page 65.

Page 100. PORTRAIT OF A POISONER. From "Central Sierra Miwok Dictionary with Texts" by Lucy Freeland and Sylvia Broadbent. *University of California Publications in Linguistics*, Vol 23. Berkeley. 1960. Page 64. The account was given by a man named Tom Williams between 1921 and 1932. Williams, who spoke the western dialect of the Central Sierra Miwok language, was living in the foothill town of Jamestown at the time.

Page 101. A FEARFUL ENCOUNTER. From "Kato Texts" by Pliny Goddard. *University of California Publications in American Archaeology and Ethnology*, Vol 5. Berkeley 1907. Page 237. The account was narrated in 1906 by Bill Ray, a man between sixty and sixty-five years old at the time.

Page 102. SEARCHING AFTER A SOUL. From "Ethnography of the Yuma Indians" by C. Darryl Forde. *University of California Publications in American Archaeology and Ethnology*, Vol 28. Berkeley. 1931. Page 193. Told by Patrick Miguel in 1929 when Miguel was in his early fifties.

Page 103. THE RAINMAKER. From "Ethnography of the Yuma Indians" by C. Darryl Forde. *University of California Publications in American Archaeology and Ethnology*, Vol 28. Berkeley. 1931. Page 197. Told by a man named Joe Homer, age sixty, in 1929.

Page 104. THE RATTLESNAKE SHAMAN. From "South Diegueño Customs" by Leslie Spier. *University of California Publications in American Archaeology and Ethnology*, Vol 20. Berkeley. 1923. Page 313. The narrator was Jim McCarthy, a man over eighty years old in 1920 when he gave this account.

Page 106. RATTLESNAKE CEREMONY SONG. From *Handbook of the Indians of California* by Alfred Kroeber. Washington: U.S. Government Printing Office. 1925. Page 506.

Page 107. THE SHAMAN AND THE CLOWN. From "Central Sierra Miwok Dictionary with Texts" by Lucy Freeland and Sylvia Broadbent. *University of California Publications in Linguistics*, Vol 23. Berkeley. 1960. Page 66. Narrated between 1921 and 1923 by Tom Williams of Jamestown.

Page 108. A GREAT AND WISE SHAMAN. From *Primitive Pragmatists* by Verne Ray. Seattle: University of Washington Press. 1963. Page 68. The narrator, Jenny Clinton, was born about 1858 on the shores of Tule Lake. At an early age she and her family were moved to Oklahoma as punishment for their participation in the Modoc War. She returned to Klamath Reservation in 1903, and gave this account in the mid-1930's.

Page 111. I DREAM OF YOU. From *Handbook of the Indians of California* by Alfred Kroeber. Washington: U.S. Government Printing Office. 1925. Page 471.

Page 113. THE DANCE OF THE SPIRITS. From "The Religion of the Luiseño and Diegueño Indians of Southern California" by Constance Du Bois. *University of California Publications in American Archaeology and Ethnology*, Vol 8 (3). Berkeley. 1908. Page 154. The story was collected at the turn of the century from an aged man, probably Salvador Cuevas, who was then a major ceremonial leader of the Luiseño.

Page 114. THE HOUSE OF SILVER-FOX. From "Achomawi Myths" by Jeremiah Curtin. *Journal of American Folklore*, Vol 22. 1909. Page 286.

Page 115. A SHAMAN'S DREAMS. From *The North American Indian*, Vol 2, by Edward Curtis. Norwood, Mass.: Plimpton Press. 1908. Page 55. Related by a shaman named Ahweyama.

Page 116. VISIT TO KUMASTAMHO. From *Handbook of the Indians of*

California by Alfred Kroeber. Washington: U.S. Government Printing Office. 1925. Page 783.

Page 119. COTTONTAIL AND THE SUN. From "Myths of the Owens Valley Paiute" by Julian Steward. *University of California Publications in American Archaeology and Ethnology*, Vol 34 (5). Berkeley. 1936. Page 371. This myth was narrated by a man named Tom Stone of Bishop.

Page 121. THE BIRTH OF THE WORLD-MAKERS. From "The Cahuilla Indians" by Lucile Hooper. *University of California Publications in American Archaeology and Ethnology*, Vol 16. Berkeley. 1920. Page 317.

Page 122. THE CREATION. From "Maidu Myths" by Roland Dixon. *Bulletin of the American Museum of Natural History*, Vol 17. Part II. New York. 1902. Page 39.

Page 123. MARUMDA AND KUKSU MAKE THE WORLD. From "Creation Myth of the Pomo Indian" by Jaime de Angulo and William Ralganal Benson. *Anthropos*, Vol 27. 1932. Page 264. The teller of the myth, William Ralganal Benson, was hereditary chief of the "Stone people" and the "Water-lily people," two Pomo subtribes who lived on the shores of Clear Lake. At the time of the telling, about 1930, Benson was more than seventy years old. The translator was Jaime de Angulo, linguist and later the author of *Indian Tales*, who more than anyone else had a fine ear for native speech and the literary talent to render it into English.

Page 127. REMAKING THE WORLD. From "Wintu Myths" by Cora Du Bois and Dorothy Demetracopoulou. *University of California Publications in American Archaeology and Ethnology*, Vol 28. Berkeley. 1931. Page 286. Told by Jenny Curl.

Page 129. WOMAN'S LOVE MEDICINE. From "Hupa Texts" by Pliny Goddard. *University of California Publications in American Archaeology and Ethnology*, Vol 1 (2). Berkeley. 1904. Page 308. The story was told by Emma Lewis in 1901. She was in her mid-fifties at the time, and had lived all her life in Hoopa Valley.

Page 131. HE-LIVES-IN-THE-SOUTH. From "Hupa Texts" by Pliny Goddard. *University of California Publications in American Archaeology and Ethnology*, Vol 1 (2). Berkeley. 1904. Page 160. Like the previous tale, told by Emma Lewis. The title is a literal translation of the foundling boy's name, Yinukatsisdai.

Page 132. THE TAR WOMAN. From "The Language of the Salinan Indians" by J. Alden Mason. *University of California Publications in American Archaeology and Ethnology*, Vol 14. Berkeley. 1918. Page 109. This myth was told by Maria Ocarpia in 1916. She was a member of the Migueleño division of the Salinan.

Page 135. A LONG TIME AGO. From "Maidu Texts and Dictionary" by William Shipley. *University of California Publications in Linguistics*, Vol 33. Berkeley. 1963. Page 61. Narrated by a woman named Maym Gallagher who lived in Payner Creek, California.

Page 137. COYOTE AND SPIDER. From "Bear River Ethnography" by Gladys Nomland. *University of California Anthropological Records*, Vol 2 (2). 1938. Page 119. The story was collected in 1928.

Page 138. COYOTE AND THE ACORNS. From "Yurok Tales" by Jean Sapir. *Journal of American Folklore*, Vol 41. 1928. Page 254. The story was narrated by a Yurok woman named Mrs. Haydom in the summer of 1927.

Page 140. COYOTE'S JOURNEY. By William Bright from *American Indian Cultural and Research Journal*, Vol 4. 1980. Page 23.

Page 146. COYOTE AND HIS GRANDMOTHER. From "Bear River Ethnography" by Gladys Nomland. *University of California Anthropological Records*, Vol 2 (2). 1938. Page 121. The story was collected in 1928.

Page 147. TWO COYOTE ADVENTURES. From "Maidu Texts" by Roland Dixon. *Publications of the American Ethnological Society*, Vol 4. Leyden, The Netherlands. 1912. Page 69. These stories were told by a man named Tom Young in 1902 or 1903. Young, who was only about thirty years old at the time, lived at Genesee in Plumas County.

Page 151. COYOTE AND BULLFISH. From "Wintu Myths" by Cora Du Bois and Dorothy Demetracopoulou. *University of California Publications in American Archaeology and Ethnology*, Vol 28. Berkeley. 1931. Page 383. Narrated by a person named Jo Bender of the Upper Sacramento River.

Page 152. COYOTE AND TRAP. From "Myths of the Owens Valley Paiute" by Julian Steward. *University of California Publications in American Archaeology and Ethnology*, Vol 34 (5). Berkeley. 1936. Page 378. The story was told by a man named Tom Stone. Stone, who lived in Bishop, was described as an "exceptionally good storyteller who immensely enjoyed his own talent."

Page 154. COYOTE STEALS FIRE. From "Myths of South Central California" by Alfred Kroeber. *University of California Publications in American Archaeology and Ethnology*, Vol 4 (4). Berkeley. 1907. Page 202.

Page 154. COYOTE AND FALCON CREATE PEOPLE. From "Myths of the South Sierra Miwok" by Samuel Barrett. *University of California Publications in American Archaeology and Ethnology*, Vol 16. Berkeley. 1919. Page 8.

Page 157. LONG AGO BROWN BEARS. From "Round Valley Songs" by William Oandasan. In *Calafia: The California Poetry*. Ishmael Reed (editor). Berkeley: Y'Bird Books. 1979. Page 259. William Oandasan, a Yuki, currently lives in New Mexico where he edits a literary journal entitled *A,* devoted largely to Native American Writing.

Page 159. THE ARRIVAL OF WHITES. From "Nomlaki Ethnography" by Walter Goldschmidt. *University of California Publications in American Archaeology and Ethnology*, Vol 42 (4). Berkeley. 1951. Page 311. The account was given by Andrew Freeman in 1936. Freeman, who was fifty-five at the time, must have heard of these incidents from people of his parents' and grandparents' generation.

Page 162. THE MASSACRE AT NEEDLE ROCK. From "Sinkyone Notes" by Gladys Nomland. *University of California Publications in American Archaeology and Ethnology*, Vol 36 (2). Berkeley. 1935. Page 166. The narrator, Sally Bell, was over ninety years old when she gave this account in 1928 or 1929. She was one of the last of the Sinkyone.

Page 164. STONE AND KELSEY MASSACRE. By William Ralganal Benson from *California Historical Society Quarterly,* Vol 11. September, 1932. Page 268. Benson, who was born in 1862, heard of these events directly from those who took part. (For more information on Benson, see footnote for page 123, "Marumda and Kuksu Make the World.")

Page 173. I NO LONGER BELIEVE. From *Primitive Pragmatists* by Verne Ray. Seattle: University of Washington Press. 1963. Page 67. The narrator, Peter Sconchin, was born in 1850 and served as one of Captain Jack's warriors. His father, John Sconchin, was second in command to Captain Jack and was hanged with him; his uncle, known generally as Old Sconchin, had been head chief of the Modoc until 1864.

Page 175. FOUR DREAM CULT SONGS. The first three songs are from "Wintu Songs" by Dorothy Demetracopoulou. *Anthropos,* Vol 30. 1935. Pages 485-487. The fourth song is from "The 1870 Ghost Dance" by Cora Du Bois. *Anthropological Records,* Vol 3 (1). Berkeley: University of California Press. 1939. Page 57. Songs 1 and 3 were sung by Sadie Marsh and Harry Marsh, respectively. Songs 2 and 4 were anonymous.

Page 177. A FISHING EXPERIENCE. From "Kashaya Texts" by Robert Oswalt. *University of California Publications in Linguistics,* Vol 36. Berkeley. 1964. Page 287. The narrator was Herman James. (See footnote for page 53, "Great Horned Owls.")

Page 180. I AM THE LAST. From *Handbook of the Yokuts Indians* by Frank Latta. Bakersfield, Calif.: Kern County Museum. 1949. Page 276. The narrator, a woman named Yoimut, died in 1933.

Page 181. I REMEMBER. By Edward Montez in *Calafia: The California Poetry.* Ishmael Reed (editor). Berkeley: Y'Bird Books. 1979. Page 250. Edward Montez was born and raised on the Cachil Dehe Rancheria on the Sacramento River, near Colusa.

Page 182. FOR THE WHITE POETS. From *Academic Squaw* by Wendy Rose. Marvin, South Dakota: Blue Cloud Quarterly. 1977. Wendy Rose, part Miwok and part Hopi, was born in Oakland in 1948. In addition to being a poet, she is an artist and an anthropologist, a graduate of the University of California at Berkeley.